passeng... 2021

4

26

48

62

74

84

features

4 Hedging the Bet
Passenger diesels of the 1960s and '70s/KEVIN J. HOLLAND

26 Ties That Bind
Passenger trains across the U.S.-Canada border/KEVIN J. HOLLAND

48 Amtrak's *North Coast Hiawatha*
A memorable 1972 trip/MIKE SCHAFER

62 Five Decades of Amtrak
A 50th anniversary photo album

74 Twilight for the M3s
Metro-North and Long Island Rail Road stalwarts/JOHN LEVAI

84 New Trains of 1951
Santa Fe, Great Northern, and some lesser lights

Cover Amtrak's *Adirondack* skirts the western shore of Lake Champlain en route from Montreal to Albany and New York City in September 1982. KEVIN EuDALY COLLECTION

PASSENGER TRAIN ANNUAL is published by
White River Productions
PO Box 48
Bucklin, MO 64631

passenger train annual 2021

Reflections

Fiftieth birthdays are always a big event, particularly when the celebrant's chances for survival have been precarious since infancy. Amtrak — an against-the-odds rail-industry survivor if ever there was one — turned 50 on May 1, 2021, culminating a half-century of tenacity and adversity. In this edition of PASSENGER TRAIN ANNUAL we explore some of the highlights of those 50 years in a decade-by-decade photo album, and with Mike Schafer's reminiscence of a 1972 trip aboard the late, lamented *North Coast Hiawatha*. Readers are encouraged to delve more deeply into Amtrak's history in the pages of our sister publication PASSENGER TRAIN JOURNAL's anniversary coverage throughout 2021.

Just as the coronavirus pandemic robbed Amtrak of what was set to be its most successful year ever in 2020, it has prevented Americans and Canadians from being able to freely cross their shared border by road or rail. International passenger-rail service in North America was already a shadow of its former glory when the pandemic caused Amtrak's *Cascades* and *Adirondack*, and the joint Amtrak-VIA *Maple Leaf*, to be suspended indefinitely from linking the two nations. As this is written in September 2021, these trains' cross-border operation had yet to resume, but readers will perhaps take some solace in this edition's cover story, "Ties That Bind," surveying some of the passenger trains that have connected the eastern U.S. and Canada, and look ahead to better times.

The final decade before Amtrak's creation saw many U.S. railroads eagerly eliminate as many of their intercity passenger trains as they could, with a few prominent holdouts bucking the trend and continuing to provide their best possible equipment and on-board service as a matter of corporate pride. With the specialized diesels acquired when these trains were new in the 1930s and '40s ripe for replacement by the mid-1960s, locomotive builders General Motors and General Electric came up with cost-effective solutions — essentially, steam-generator-equipped freight models — that gave a fresh face to some of the nation's best-known streamliners, and were far more affordable than reviving dormant production lines to replicate their cab and booster predecessors. "Hedging the Bet" examines the motive power solutions developed by the builders, and looks at how these mostly unstreamlined locomotives paved the way for later generations of passenger power.

On the transit front, author and photographer John Levai looks at the twilight of M3 electric-multiple-unit train operation in New York City. These familiar trainsets have run their last revenue miles on MTA component Long Island Rail Road, but survive, for the time being, on Metro-North.

We continue our recurring "New Trains" coverage with a visit to 1951, a year in which two premier trains — Santa Fe's *Super Chief* and Great Northern's *Empire Builder* — were re-equipped for the second time in the postwar era. GN's *Western Star* was another headline maker in a year that saw relatively few other infusions of new passenger equipment, but did include a group of 16 no-frills commuter coaches built by Budd for New York, Susquehanna & Western.

Finally, a note of thanks to Nick Fry, curator of the Barriger National Railroad Library at the Mercantile Library, University of Missouri St. Louis, and to WRP colleague Otto Vondrak for their assistance in providing photographs for this edition of PASSENGER TRAIN ANNUAL.

Kevin J. Holland **editor**

publisher
Kevin EuDaly/White River Productions

editor and art director
Kevin J. Holland

senior editor
Mike Schafer

contributing editor
Kevin McKinney

dealer sales
Dan Hansen

circulation manager
Nadean EuDaly

production technician
Kevin J. Holland

proofreader
Julie Jessup

editorial address
passenger train annual
4145 Lakeshore Road, Suite 22
Burlington, ON Canada L7L 1A3
kholland@passengertrainjournal.com

© Copyright 2021 by White River Productions, PO Box 48, Bucklin, MO 64631. All Rights Reserved. Printed in the U.S.A. The contents of this publication may not be reproduced in part or in whole without the prior written permission of the publisher or editor.

ISBN 978-1-932804-73-0

PTA21

from the publisher of

With snow-covered Mount Shasta in the distance, Amtrak's *Coast Starlight* rolls through northern California's Siskiyou County in October 2004. DAN MUNSON

Hedging

For North American passenger trains i

BY KEVIN J. HOLLAND ©2021

Streamlined diesel locomotives first appeared in the United States in the 1930s, at a time when new forms of railroad motive power and passenger rolling stock were changing both the appearance and the economics of the nation's passenger trains, and as public tastes in design progressed beyond Art Deco toward its even-more-refined 1940s offspring, Moderne.

Fast forward to the late 1950s, when any North American diesel-powered passenger train still worth its advertising budget was powered by matched sets of streamlined cab and booster units. Many of these locomotives were beginning to show their age, however, and the declining fortunes of most passenger-train operations meant that U.S. railroads weren't inclined to spend money on in-kind replacements of these specialized and relatively expensive diesels. Indeed, most U.S. railroads by the mid-1960s were doing their utmost to get rid of passenger trains entirely, and that had led diesel builders to drop these choices (costly to build and to buy) from their catalogs.

A face made for freight: Three U28CG units lead Santa Fe's *Texas Chief* in July 1968. JIM BOYD; KEVIN EuDALY COLLECTION

the Bet

...e 1960s and '70s, a triumph of substance over style

Alco (and its partner at the time, General Electric) had built the last PA/PB cab and booster types back in 1953, and affiliate Montreal Locomotive Works (MLW) delivered the last FPA/FPBs in 1959. The Electro-Motive Division of General Motors (EMD) delivered its final passenger-service FP7 in 1953, its final FP9 in 1959 (from Canadian subsidiary GMD), and its last E-units in 1963.

The handful of 1960s pro-passenger holdouts — led by Santa Fe, Seaboard Air Line, Great Northern, and Union Pacific — faced a real dilemma. Even though these roads maintained a high standard of passenger service, the future of the railroad-operated passenger train was bleak, and replacing their steam-generator-equipped diesel rosters with a new generation of E- or F-units — even if the builders were willing — made little economic sense. The solution, for these roads and a handful of others (including the virulently anti-passenger Southern Pacific), was to hedge the bet by acquiring modified freight models at minimal added cost which, in the worst case, could easily be reassigned to freight service if and when the passenger market collapsed.

In response to this emerging (but small) market, U.S. diesel locomotive builders added variants of their medium- and high-horsepower second-generation freight models to their catalogs.

GP30B and GP35

Even before building its final E9 cab and booster units in December 1963 (for Union Pacific), EMD got the next-generation 1960s passenger power parade going when it delivered 13 boiler-equipped GP30B units to UP in the summer of 1963 (numbered 727B-739B, within a larger UP order for a total of 40 of these cabless hump-roofed hood units).

And in an evolution of its first-generation passenger-service GP and SD units (which could house steam generators in their high-hood noses), EMD built 15 boiler-equipped, high-hood GP35s for Nacionales de Mexico (NdeM) in late 1964. These Mexican units were delivered as numbers 8215-8229, and were the first in a long line of second-generation road switchers acquired for passenger service south of the border.

C-420

The Century Series was Alco's answer to EMD's expanding range of second-generation models, with the C-420 introduced as a catalog successor to the

TOP EMD's ungainly GP30B offered plenty of space for a steam generator in its forward end. Union Pacific acquired the only boiler-equipped GP30Bs in mid-1963. UP 738B was at Denver on August 26, 1965. CHUCK ZEILER

ABOVE Nacionales de Mexico's GP35s 8215-8229 were EMD's first cab-equipped second-generation road switchers built with steam generators for passenger service. NdeM 8225 was at San Luis Potosi in 1966. ROGER PUTA

BELOW Long Island Rail Road acquired 30 Alco C-420s equipped with steam generators in their high-hood noses between 1963 and 1968. LIRR 221 wore its original paint at Jamaica, N.Y., in June 1968. MIKE SCHAFER

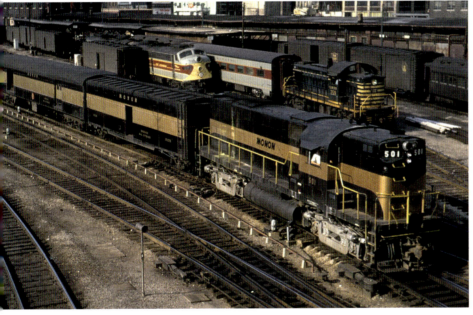

TOP **The rear end of SAL SDP35 1111 in March 1965, showing the steam-generator compartment, and end platform and steps modified from EMD's standard practice.** RAY COOK; KEVIN EuDALY COLLECTION

ABOVE **SAL SDP35 1117 at Atlanta's Terminal Station in July 1967.** KEVIN EuDALY COLLECTION

LEFT **Monon C-420 501 leads the *Thoroughbred* at Chicago in August 1967.** KEVIN EuDALY COLLECTION

RS-11 and RS-36. In December 1963, Long Island Rail Road took delivery of the first of an eventual 30 steam-generator-equipped C-420 units, numbered LIRR 200-229. Twenty-two units were on the property by July 1964, and a final batch of eight arrived in 1968.

The only other railroad to acquire new steam-generator-equipped C-420s was Monon, with a pair built in August 1966 to replace F-units on the *Thoroughbred* between Chicago and Louisville. After Monon's last passenger train was discontinued in September 1967, C-420s 501 and 502 joined the freight pool.

SDP35

Next up from EMD for the U.S. market was the SDP35, introduced in 1964 and establishing the builder's practice of providing space at the rear of low-nose units for a steam generator and related equipment. Built on a standard SD35 frame and sharing that model's 60' 8" length over couplers, the SDP35's major components were shifted forward, and the rear platform and steps modified, to accommodate the additional equipment.

The "P" in SDP35 indicated a boiler-equipped unit for Passenger service. The first customer for the new model was Seaboard Air Line Railroad (SAL), which needed to replace the oldest E-units (many of which dated to the late 1930s and '40s) that led its Florida streamliners. The SDP35's nominally higher horsepower (2,500 hp from a single 567-series engine, vs. 2,400 hp for a twin-engined E9) offered the distinct benefit of reduced maintenance.

EMD built a total of 35 SDP35s between July 1964 and September 1965, for SAL (20); Atlantic Coast Line (a single unit); Union Pacific (10); and Louisville & Nashville (four).

Seaboard's large fleet (delivered as SAL 1100-1119) performed double duty in fast main line passenger service as well as powering piggyback trains and other priority freight traffic. With the July 1967 merger of SAL and ACL to create Seaboard Coast Line, the ex-SAL SDP35s initially were renumbered as SCL 601-620, and were joined by ex-ACL 1099 (built as ACL 550), which became SCL 600.

Louisville & Nashville's SDP35 units ended up being delivered without steam generators, after L&N passenger-train discontinuances that occurred while the locomotives were under construction rendered the boilers unnecessary. Although as a result they lacked the telltale rooftop vents at the rear of the long hood, the four L&N units (delivered as 1700-1703) did retain the related hood-side air-intake openings and distinctive beveled bulge on the left side of the steam-generator compartment.

Union Pacific, which was operating some E9s that were only a few months older than its SDP35s, soon determined that the latter type was better suited to freight service and permanently reassigned its 10 units (UP 1400-1409).

SDP40

This model debuted in mid-1966 as a boiler-equipped variant of EMD's 3,000-hp SD40 freight model. Like the earlier SDP35, the SDP40 was built on a standard-length frame, with the SD40's mechanical and body components shifted forward and the steam-generator equipment housed in an elongated hood that extended onto what would have been the standard SD40's rear platform and step area.

The only U.S. customer for the SDP40 was Great Northern, which acquired six (numbered 320-325) in May 1966 for use on the *Western Star*, the *Internationals*, and other secondary trains. These units became Burlington Northern 9850-9855 at the time of the March 1970 BN merger, and were later renumbered as BN 6394-6399.

Notably, in April 1975 BN SDP40 6397 was renumbered 1976 and repainted in a special livery celebrating

TOP **SCL SDP35 1958's steam generator had been removed (along with its left-side hood bulge) by the time of this 1977 view at Sharonville, Ohio. This unit was built as SAL 1107.** DAN DOVER; KEVIN J. HOLLAND COLLECTION

ABOVE **Louisville & Nashville's four SDP35s were ordered with, but delivered without, steam generators. L&N 1700 was photographed in August 1966.** KEVIN J. HOLLAND COLLECTION

BELOW **Union Pacific 1401 and a sister, at Council Bluffs, Iowa, in October 1965, show the differing left and right sides of the steam-generator compartment at the rear of the SDP35.** LOU SCHMITZ; CHUCK ZEILER COLLECTION

ABOVE Great Northern's *Western Star* pauses at Wenatchee, Wash., in August 1968 behind a pair of SDP40s. The trailing unit has been repainted in GN's recently introduced Big Sky Blue image. STAN STYLES; KEVIN EuDALY COLLECTION

RIGHT Fresh from EMD's factory in suburban Chicago, GN SDP40 325 makes its delivery trip over Burlington Route in 1966. JIM BOYD; KEVIN EuDALY COLLECTION

BELOW SDP40s 325 and 324 lead GN Train 27, the St. Paul–Seattle *Western Star*, at Whitefish, Mont., on March 1, 1968. The first car in the train is a steam-generator unit augmenting the boilers in the two locomotives. It was one of several rebuilt from retired F3B units, and known as heater cars on GN.
TIM MORRIS; KEVIN EuDALY COLLECTION

the U.S. bicentennial, five years after the unit had seen its last regular passenger service.

Fourteen SDP40s were delivered to NdeM in 1968 (numbered 8522-8531) and 1970 (built as NdeM 8532-8535), yielding a total production run of only 20 units for this model.

Even more so than had been the case when an SDP35 replaced older E- or F-units, with the 3,000-hp SDP40 fewer locomotives were needed to power an equivalent train at the required schedule speeds, while still promising lower maintenance and fuel costs vs. the obsolete generation of locomotives.

ABOVE **NdeM SDP40 8523 at San Luis Potosi in December 1986.** JOHN C. BENSON; KEVIN J. HOLLAND COLLECTION

RIGHT **In familiar territory, two leased Southern Pacific SDP45s lead Amtrak's *Coast Daylight* at San Luis Obispo, Calif., in July 1973. SDP45s shared the SD45's flared radiator design.** NICK MUFF; KEVIN EuDALY COLLECTION

BELOW **SP's SDP45 fleet was also employed on the road's San Francisco commuter operation beginning in 1971. SP 3202 rests with Train 118 in the terminal at Third and Townsend streets on December 24, 1971.** GEORGE H. DRURY

BOTTOM RIGHT **After CalTrain took over the San Francisco commuter service in 1985, SP maintained the steam generators in SDP45s 3207 and 3201 for assignment to occasional special-event trains.** RICHARD YAREMKO

SDP45

EMD had more success with the 3,600-hp SDP45, introduced in May 1967, but the production total of 52 units is somewhat deceptive. Taking advantage of the increased fuel capacity available beneath the SDP45's extended frame (some five feet longer than the SD45), Erie Lackawanna acquired 34 units between May 1969 and August 1970 for freight service between New Jersey and Chicago, with the goal of eliminating fueling stops between endpoints. EL's SDP45 fleet lacked steam generators, and although their hoods were longer than a standard SD45, they were distinguished by having EMD's usual beveled rear end, without the rectangular air vent on each side of the boxy passenger-service variant.

The largest fleet of boiler-equipped SDP45s — 10 in total — was acquired by Southern Pacific in mid-1967. Numbered 3200-3209, they were intended for SP's long-haul trains but also saw regional service in the San Joaquin Valley. During its early years, Amtrak leased

TOP **Reflecting Great Northern's post-1967 Big Sky Blue identity, two GN SDP45s and a cowl-bodied F45 (the latter model not equipped with a steam generator) await their call on the *Empire Builder* at Havre, Mont., on September 1, 1969.** GEORGE H. DRURY

ABOVE **GN SDP45s 328 and 329 are ready for their next assignment at Minneapolis, Minn., on June 1, 1968.** ALAN MILLER; KEVIN EuDALY COLLECTION

LEFT **Following their absorption into Burlington Northern's freight roster, the ex-GN SDP45s received new numbers and Cascade Green paint. BN 6598 (originally GN 332) leads an SD45 on a freight in September 1974.** ALAN MILLER; KEVIN EuDALY COLLECTION

five SDP45s for use on its SP routes. After 1971, SDP45s also saw service on SP's San Francisco Peninsula commuter trains, where they hastened the demise of SP's celebrated Fairbanks-Morse H24-66 "Train Master" locomotives.

The only other SDP45 buyer, Great Northern, took delivery of eight, numbered 326-333, in the summer of 1967 for assignment to the *Empire Builder*. Unlike GN's SDP40s, which were delivered in the road's classic Omaha Orange and green paint, the SDP45s' arrival coincided with the 1967 introduction of Great Northern's Big Sky Blue corporate identity. All but one of the earlier SDP40s also received blue paint (number 323 was the holdout).

GN's SDP45s became Burlington Northern 9856-9863 in March 1970 and were later renumbered BN 6592-6599.

GP40TC

EMD's Canadian affiliate, General Motors Diesel (GMD) of London, Ont., introduced GM's first customized four-axle second-generation passenger model when it delivered eight GP40TC units for Toronto-area commuter start-up GO Transit in 1966. (The "TC" in the model designation indicated Toronto Commuter.) These were doubly notable as being the first of GM's growing family of passenger-service hood units to include a head-end power (HEP) generator instead of a steam generator. HEP was provided by a GM 12-149 V-type engine driving a GE ATI-740 series alternator.

The GP40TC units were delivered in late 1966, several months before GO was ready to begin service. In the interim, bearing small Canadian National logos, they were placed in CN freight service. Originally numbered as GO 600-607 (later 9800-9807 and 500-507), their push-pull passenger careers began in May 1967.

The GP40TC design combined an SD40 frame and the mechanical components of a standard GP40, with an extended rear hood housing the HEP equipment. With the short range of their

ABOVE GO Transit's eight GP40TC units were built on SD40 frames, and were Canada's first HEP-equipped diesels. Delivered in late 1966 before GO started operations, they ran in CN freight service with partial GO paint and CN markings until May 1967. GO 605 is at CN's Hamilton, Ont., yard in this March 15, 1967, view. DOUG WINGFIELD

BELOW GO GP40TC 9807 (originally 607) leads its train into Toronto Union Station in 1974. GEORGE H. DRURY

BOTTOM LEFT The GP40TCs were rebuilt in 1975 with modified HEP packages, and emerged in this green-and-white livery. A year later, GO 9800-9807 were renumbered 500-507. In this June 1980 view, GO 507 pushes a Hamilton-bound bilevel train at Bayview Junction, Ont. ROBERT FARKAS; KEN GOSLETT COLLECTION

BOTTOM RIGHT Amtrak bought all eight GP40TCs in October 1988. Leading Train 68, the *Adirondack*, at Glenville, N.Y., in May 1994, Amtrak 198 was originally GO Transit 606. JOHN BARTLEY; KEVIN EuDALY COLLECTION

intended suburban operations, the units were built with relatively small 1,000-gallon fuel tanks.

After 21 years in GO Transit service, during which their rear hoods were modified in 1975 to accommodate a revised, sound-insulated HEP installation, all eight GP40TC units were sold to Amtrak in October 1988.

Amtrak put its redesignated GP40PH units (numbered 192-199, and later 520-527) to work powering Eastern and Midwestern regional and long-distance trains. Rebuilt in 2004-05 as GP38H-3 units (with their horsepower reduced from 3,000 to 2,000), they are still employed in Amtrak work-train service and as standby power in the Northeast.

GP40P

In 1968, EMD produced another GP40 variant for commuter service, this time as the steam-generator-equipped GP40P for Central of New Jersey (CNJ). Thirteen units were delivered as CNJ 3671-3783.

Not only did the GP40P incorporate EMD's now-standard rear hood extension, but the low-nosed model also featured SD45-style flared radiators, to create enough internal space for the steam-generator equipment.

Built for use on CNJ's Raritan Valley and North Jersey Coast lines, purchase of the 13 units was funded by the New Jersey Department of Transportation, and as delivered the units wore CNJ blue paint with small NJDOT logos on their steam-generator compartments. NJDOT took over the commuter operation when CNJ became part of Conrail in 1976, and renumbered the GP40Ps as 4100-4112. At this time they began to appear in NJDOT's dark blue and silver paint.

In 1980, NJ Transit's "disco stripe" silver and black livery became the new standard, retaining the units' previous NJDOT numbers.

In the mid-1980s, NJ Transit's GP40Ps had their steam generators replaced with HEP equipment, and were redesignated GP40PHs as a result.

TOP **Central of New Jersey took delivery of 13 GP40P units for commuter service in 1968.** ROGER PUTA

ABOVE **With its CNJ lettering painted over, GP40P 4105 carries a new NJDOT number at South Amboy, N.J., in December 1978. Flared SD45-style radiators, combined with the rear hood extension and modified rear platform and steps, were distinctive features of the GP40P.** J.C. SMITH; KEVIN J. HOLLAND COLLECTION

BELOW **GP40P 4100 wears NJ Transit's full "disco stripe" livery at Raritan, N.J., in September 1980. Within a few years, these units' steam generators were replaced with HEP.** RICHARD LOUDERBACK; KEVIN J. HOLLAND COLLECTION

Meanwhile, on Santa Fe

Among the staunchest of pro-passenger U.S. railroads in the 1960s, Santa Fe opted to rejuvenate its passenger locomotive pool (made up mostly of aging F-units) beginning in 1966 with a mix of second-generation road switcher and cowl-body models from EMD and GE.

The first to appear, in the summer of 1966, were ten U28CG units from GE, which from trackside were largely indistinguishable from the builder's standard U28C freight model. The steam generator (accounting for the G in the model designation) was housed in a compartment immediately aft of the cab which, correctly sensing a potential market, GE's designers had provided in all of the company's latest versions of its growing line of Universal-series models (unofficially dubbed "U-Boats" by many observers). The U28CG was the first GE model to actually employ a steam generator in this available space, with the related vents and air intakes visible on the roof and hood sides behind the cab, and a bulge in the left-side hood behind the cab, the only external structural evidence of the unit's passenger-service status.

Cosmetically, Santa Fe's practice of painting passenger and freight diesels in distinct schemes cleared up any uncertainty over these red-and-silver "Warbonnet" units' intended assignments.

Santa Fe 350-359 were the only examples of the U28CG to be built, and they were assigned to the *Texas Chief* and other secondary trains.

Santa Fe returned to GE a year later for a group of six distinctive U30CG units. This model, also acquired only by Santa Fe, housed the mechanical innards of a steam-generator-equipped U30C inside a non-structural cowl body, which eliminated the optical stigma of road switchers leading Santa

ABOVE Two U28CGs lead the *Texas Chief* in June 1966. Red pilots on these newly delivered units soon gave way to silver paint. JIM BOYD; KEVIN EuDALY COLLECTION

BELOW The *Texas Chief* arriving at Chicago behind consecutively numbered U28CGs in October 1967. Large lettering was a departure from Santa Fe's "Warbonnet" passenger-service standard. A wisp of steam behind the lead unit's cab roof indicates the location of the steam-generator compartment. JIM BOYD; KEVIN EuDALY COLLECTION

OPPOSITE TOP **U28CG 350 arrives at San Diego, Calif., with a southbound *San Diegan* from Los Angeles in September 1968.** IMRE QUASTLER; KEVIN EuDALY COLLECTION

OPPOSITE MIDDLE **Following a February 1969 derailment, Santa Fe temporarily reassigned its U28CG and U30CG units to freight service. In June 1969, examples of both models lead this freight train at Chicago.** JIM BOYD; KEVIN EuDALY COLLECTION

OPPOSITE BOTTOM **Cowl-bodied U30CG 401 leads two U28CGs out of Chicago in August 1969. Santa Fe reverted to small lettering of its name on the sides of these "Warbonnet" cowl units.** JIM BOYD; KEVIN EuDALY COLLECTION

ABOVE **U30CG 404 leads a short westbound train at Edelstein, Ill., in August 1968.** J. HARLEN WILSON COLLECTION

Fe's passenger trains. Santa Fe 400-405 were delivered in November 1967 wearing the road's traditional "Warbonnet" paint, without the large road name lettering used on the earlier U28CG units. The U30CG units' principal assignment was the *Grand Canyon Limited* linking Los Angeles and Chicago, and they also saw service on the *Texas Chief*, *Tulsan*, and *San Diegans*.

Despite their mechanical and cosmetic specialization for passenger service, and Santa Fe's ongoing need for new passenger power, the U30CGs were reassigned to freight service following a February 1969 derailment of the *Grand Canyon Limited* that raised concerns over the GE trucks' stability at passenger speeds. Riding on the same truck design, the U28CGs were caught up in the same cautionary reassignment.

Santa Fe's boiler-equipped GE units saw a return to passenger service by the end of 1969, but for the most part spent the rest of their careers in freight service. In April 1970 the U30CGs were renumbered 8000-8005, and the U28CGs became numbers 7900-7909.

In December 1967, Santa Fe received nine examples of the FP45 from EMD — essentially, an SDP45 with a nonstructural cowl body. Numbered 100-108 and wearing "Warbonnet" paint, they served alongside a larger fleet of 40

F45 cowl units wearing a more somber Santa Fe livery in freight service.

Although some F-units soldiered on until the end of Santa Fe passenger service, the U28CG, U30CG, and FP45 units were the modern face of the company's passenger operations. Retained by Santa Fe after Amtrak's debut, the FP45s were repurposed as fast freight units, leading the *Super C* and other premier intermodal trains. Before their steam generators were removed, they also pinch-hit when Amtrak was short of power for its former Santa Fe trains.

Cowls to the Twin Cities and Omaha

The Milwaukee Road acquired five FP45 units in 1969 to replace increasingly infirm E-units on its fast *Hiawatha* schedules between Chicago and Minneapolis-St. Paul, Minn., and on the *City* streamliners operated jointly with Union Pacific east of Omaha, Neb. Delivered in Armour Yellow (a legacy of the railroad's post-1955 status as the eastern link in UP's Chicago–West Coast Overland Route operations) and numbered 1-5, the FP45s led passenger trains for barely two years before Amtrak's arrival, at which time they were retained by Milwaukee Road, repainted, and placed in freight service.

Cowls to the Crescent City?

One pro-passenger railroad that almost became a member of the 1960s "cowl club" was Illinois Central. Facing the same motive-power dilemma as other roads that were commited, whether

ABOVE **After being temporarily withdrawn from passenger service in 1969, Santa Fe's passenger-service U-Boats were permanently reassigned to freight duties following Amtrak's creation. In March 1980, U30CG 8005 (originally numbered 405) leads a freight train in Texas.** BILL PHILLIPS; KEVIN EuDALY COLLECTION

BELOW **A steam-generator-equipped Santa Fe FP45 and a boilerless F45 (both renumbered from their delivery series) prepare to lead Amtrak's *Chief* out of Chicago's Dearborn Station in May 1971.** PHIL GOSNEY

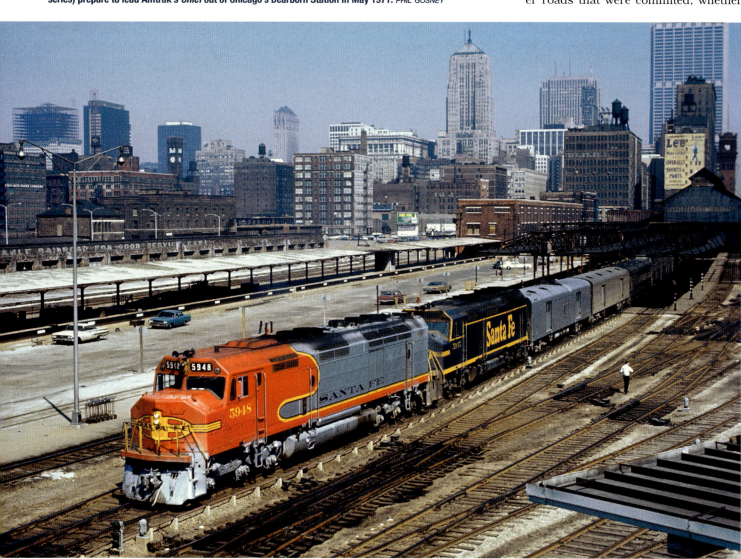

by choice or by statute, to continued operation of passenger trains, IC gave serious thought to acquiring five FP45s to augment its orange-and-brown E-units. An order slot was confirmed by EMD, and serial numbers were assigned, but the units were never built. That decision ended the fleeting prospect of cowl units at the head of the *Panama Limited* or *City of New Orleans*, at least in the pre-Amtrak era.

U-Boats for the *CZ*?

Western Pacific's orange and silver F-units were a hallmark of that road's *California Zephyr* partnership, with WP operating the Bay Area-to-Chicago domeliner between Oakland, Calif., and Salt Lake City. In a situation playing out across the country, however, by the late 1960s WP's passenger F-units were the better part of two decades old and increasingly costly to maintain. WP management concluded that, with a steam-generator car providing heat for the trailing consist, freight diesels geared for passenger speeds could solve the problem of repowering a train the company also happened to be trying to discontinue. Any diesels acquired under such an arrangement could be immediately sent to the freight pool when their passenger assignment was over.

GE delivered a group of ten U30Bs in 1969 (WP 760-769), equipped with passenger signal lines and clad in the same orange and silver colors of the F-units

TOP **Milwaukee Road FP45s lead the "City of Everywhere" on June 4, 1969.** JIM BOYD; KEVIN EuDALY COLLECTION

ABOVE **Externally, the FP45 was distinguished from the shorter F45 by the steam-generator compartment aft of the radiator grilles. Milwaukee Road 2 is shown at Chicago in March 1969.** JIM BOYD; KEVIN EuDALY COLLECTION

BELOW **Western Pacific ordered ten U30Bs (WP 760-769) to replace F-units on the *California Zephyr*, but test trips showed they were unsuited for the assignment and the plan was shelved.** JIM BOYD; KEVIN EuDALY COLLECTION

passenger train annual 2021 **19**

they were intended to replace. WP's goal was to replace three F-units with a single U30B. The plan was shelved after test-trip evaluation showed that a single U-Boat was hard-pressed to reliably maintain the *CZ*'s schedule speeds of up to 79 mph, and assigning two U-Boats to the train would have been uneconomical. WP's venerable F-units carried on, sometimes in the company of a steam-generator car, until the *California Zephyr* was discontinued as a through train on March 22, 1970.

North of the border

Canadian National and Canadian Pacific were polar opposites on the subject of rail passenger service in the 1960s. While CP was actively trying to jettison its few remaining intercity passenger trains, CN took a more pragmatic and progressive approach, influenced partly by its federal mandate as a publicly owned company to serve unremunerative markets, and partly by the desire of management at the time to determine conclusively whether or not the passenger train had any chance of a profitable future. In parallel with its commitment to introducing the TurboTrain, CN unveiled Canada's first HEP-equipped intercity trains when Tempo service debuted in southwestern Ontario in June 1968.

A fleet of 25 new aluminum-bodied Tempo cars was built by Hawker Siddeley, but rather than acquire new HEP-equipped locomotives (as GO Transit had done just over a year before), CN opted to rebuild six MLW RS-18 road switchers (essentially, the Canadian version of Alco's RS-11). These units already had full-height noses, and these were extended forward onto the front platform to accommodate new HEP engine-generator equipment. As had been the case with GO's GP40TCs, the rebuilt RS-18M units were completed before their accompanying cars were ready, and they were placed in freight service. Intriguingly, they were outshopped wearing CN's obsolete pre-1961 green-and-yellow diesel colors, an early (and officially undeclared) nod to "heritage"

LEFT **CN extended the noses of six RS-18 freight units in 1967 to accommodate HEP equipment. By the time of this 1978 view in VIA service, RS-18M 3153 had lost its HEP package due to a wreck, but kept its extended nose.** JIM BOYD; KEVIN EuDALY COLLECTION

BELOW **A pre-inaugural Tempo train at Toronto Union Station in May 1968. Service commenced the following month.** JIM BOYD; KEVIN EuDALY COLLECTION

RIGHT **C-424s were a common sight on some of CN's passenger trains in the Maritime provinces as well as in northern Ontario and Quebec. With a steam-generator car in tow, these C-424s lead a Montreal–Halifax train at Moncton, N.B., in 1972.** KEN GOSLETT

BELOW RIGHT **CN GP40 4016 and a steam-generator unit lead an eastbound train at Guelph, Ont., in 1973.** KEVIN J. HOLLAND COLLECTION

liveries. With Tempo service set to begin in the spring of 1968, the six RS-18M units were sent back to Montreal for repainting in their official livery, a striking adaptation of CN's 1961 palette featuring a mostly red-orange body and white cab. CN Tempo service proved popular, but failed as a proof-of-concept for wider implementation. Accidents resulted in two of the units losing their HEP equipment, which was reinstalled in rebuilt baggage cars for greater motive-power flexibility. Following the creation of VIA Rail Canada, the RS-18Ms were leased by VIA from CN and continued in Tempo service in their full CN colors until all six were retired in 1983 and scrapped.

In 1967, around the same time that it was rebuilding the RS-18s for Tempo service, CN acquired a group of 16 GP40s from GMD. The last two of the order, CN 4016 and 4017 (later 9316-9317), were geared for passenger-train speeds and served regional routes in southwestern Ontario into the VIA era.

In eastern Canada, CN also assigned second-generation road switchers including C-424s, C-630s, GP40-2Ws, and M-420s to periodic passenger duties.

passenger train annual 2021   21

ABOVE In the first month of Auto-Train operation, two U36Bs are at Lorton, Va., in December 1971. GEORGE H. DRURY

RIGHT Led by two U36Bs, a southbound Auto-Train crosses an inlet of the Potomac River at Neabsco, Va., shortly after departing the company's Lorton, Va., terminal in March 1974. GEORGE H. DRURY

Auto-Train

Seven months after Amtrak profoundly altered the U.S. passenger-train landscape, the highly improbable happened when a new privately operated long-distance train service debuted on December 6, 1971. Linking suburban Washington, D.C. (Lorton, Va.), with central Florida (where Walt Disney World had opened five weeks before), Auto-Train moved passengers and their automobiles with an overnight schedule that included plenty of dome cars as well as distinctive motive power.

Employing secondhand steam-generator cars to heat its car fleet, Auto-Train opted for GE's compact and powerful U36B to power the trains. Painted in an eye-catching white, purple, and red scheme to match the trailing auto

22 passenger train annual 2021

carriers and passenger cars, the 13 Auto-Train U36Bs (numbered 4000-4012) were built to host-railroad Seaboard Coast Line specifications, right down to their trade-in Blomberg trucks (an EMD standard that was uncommon under other builders' products). They were freight units, inside and out, with no mechanical alterations for passenger duty. A 1974 order for four additional units was overtaken by Auto-Train's mounting financial problems and was canceled, with these locomotives delivered by GE as Conrail 2971-2974, riding on standard AAR Type B trucks.

Into the Amtrak era

The decision by Amtrak management to acquire EMD's 3,000-hp SDP40F beginning in 1973 — essentially a lengthened, cowl-bodied SD40-2 — involved a degree of "bet hedging." In the event that Amtrak failed — not beyond the realm of possibility at the time — the suddenly surplus SDP40F fleet, designed with easily removable dual steam generators, would have been offered to freight railroads.

As events transpired, the SDP40Fs *did* have relatively short Amtrak careers, but not because of politics. Problems with weight distribution and running gear made them prone to derailments entering main line curves under specific circumstances. After schedule-hindering speed restrictions (and some outright bans) were placed on the units by many of Amtrak's host railroads, most of the SDP40F fleet was traded back to EMD. The F40PH, initially acquired by Amtrak as a short-haul locomotive to operate with HEP-equipped Amfleet cars, was repurposed to also serve long-haul routes, and became the core of Amtrak's systemwide diesel roster for almost two decades. Major SDP40F components were salvaged by EMD for use in replacement F40PHR units. Fulfilling the alternate career originally envisioned as a possibility for the SDP40F, 18 of the units did find their way into freight service on Santa Fe in 1984 as the SDF40-2.

LEFT Amtrak SDP40F 508 in *San Diegan* service at San Diego, Calif., in August 1973. With Amtrak's future unclear at the time, this model was designed for quick conversion to freight use. KEVIN EuDALY COLLECTION

BELOW Acquired from Amtrak in 1984 in exchange for 43 surplus Santa Fe switcher and work-train locomotives, 18 retired SDP40Fs were converted to SDF40-2 freight units (Santa Fe 5250-5267). KEVIN EuDALY COLLECTION

ABOVE With funding from New Jersey's Department of Transportation, Erie Lackawanna acquired 32 U34CH units between October 1970 and January 1973. U34CH 3355 is shown in NJDOT colors at Hoboken, N.J., in March 1977. KEVIN EuDALY COLLECTION

LEFT Shown in San Francisco commuter service in October 1975, Southern Pacific GP40P-2 3197 was one of three SP system diesels to receive bicentennial paint. After being reassigned to freight service in 1985 and having their steam generators removed, SP's three GP40P-2s (the only examples built) were renumbered 7600-7602. KEVIN EuDALY COLLECTION

BELOW SP's three GP40P-2 units arrived in 1974 to complete the motive-power re-equipping of its San Francisco commuter operation. SP 3199 was en route west from EMD at Riverdale, Ill., in November 1974. PAUL HUNNELL; KEVIN EuDALY COLLECTION

ABOVE An overhead view of Metra F40C 604. Developed for Chicago commuter service in 1974, the HEP-equipped F40C was EMD's last six-axle cowl locomotive. DENNIS HERTRICH; KEVIN EuDALY COLLECTION

TOP RIGHT Only 15 F40C units were built before the F40PH found favor with Chicago's Regional Transit Authority (precursor to Metra), and with other urban operators in the U.S. and Canada. In this February 1985 view, F40C 45 pushes a commuter train toward Chicago Union Station. KEVIN EuDALY COLLECTION

RIGHT Nacionales de Mexico acquired two groups of GP38P-2 units, with steam generators in their noses. The first 20 (NdeM 9200-9219) arrived in June 1975, with 9901-9909 following seven years later. NdeM was also the only customer for GE's U36CG, taking 20 of that model in 1974. JOHN C. BENSON; KEVIN J. HOLLAND COLLECTION

The SDP40Fs were Amtrak's first new diesel locomotives, and proved to be the company's only ones built with steam generators (although the GE E60CP electrics also had them). The SDP40F design included provision for installation of HEP equipment to replace the twin steam generators, but this was never done.

Ill-starred as they were, the SDP40Fs weren't quite the culmination of EMD's six-axle cowl-unit evolution, begun in 1967 with the FP45.

More suburban power

On the commuter front, modified road switchers continued to find favor with operators on both coasts. In the New York City area, Erie-Lackawanna and NJDOT cooperated to acquire and operate a fleet of 32 U34CH units for service out of Hoboken, N.J. Delivered between 1970 and 1973, GE's U34CH was a 3,450-hp HEP-equipped variant (and precursor) of the U36C, with a portion of its power output devoted to the cars' electrical requirements. They remained in service until 1994.

In San Francisco, Southern Pacific received three GP40P-2 units in 1974 (SP 3197-3199) to augment the SDP45s used in Peninsula commuter service since 1971, bringing down the final curtain on the last H24-66 "Train Masters" used in that operation. Like the earlier GP40P built for CNJ, the Dash-2 version employed SD45-style flared radiators. After CalTrain assumed operating responsibility for SP's commuter service in 1985, the GP40P-2 and SDP45 units were reassigned to freight duties.

In Chicago, EMD delivered 15 F40C cowl units in 1974 to the two commuter agencies providing service on Milwaukee Road lines (the North West Suburban Mass Transit District and the North Suburban Mass Transit District, both eventually absorbed by the Regional Transit Authority and, later, by Metra). With a design based on the SDP40F, the 3½-foot-shorter F40C produced 3,200 hp and featured unusual "jalousie" louvered stainless-steel side panels. Having survived long enough to see Metra service (but always assigned to ex-Milwaukee Road lines), all but two of the F40Cs were retired by 2004, with the survivors seeing intermittent service for several more years.

The trend continues

On the heels of the U34CH, F40C and GP40P-2, the mid-1970s and '80s brought new crops of cowl and road-switcher diesel models in passenger service. Ranging from Amtrak's P30CH and F40PH models and NdeM's GP38P-2s to a host of new and remanufactured types for U.S. and Canadian commuter agencies, these locomotives will be surveyed in a future edition of *Passenger Train Annual*.

Adirondack

Atlantic Limited

International Limited

Ties That

A look back at some of the

Since the early days of railroad surveying and construction in North America, the boundary between the United States and Canada has often been more of a political impediment than a practical one.

Recognizing that their economic fortunes were largely intertwined, builders of the two nations' burgeoning rail networks reached across the border whenever, and wherever, it made sense to do so, both physically and managerially.

With steel ties thus established, freight and passenger traffic crossed what was long regarded as the "world's longest undefended border" with increasing frequency. For passengers during the heyday of 20th century rail travel, this

Bind

Passenger trains linking the eastern U.S. and Canada

BY KEVIN J. HOLLAND ©2021

meant convenient coach and sleeping-car service linking U.S. and Canadian communities, large and small, either aboard through trains or interline cars.

Although these ties dwindled in the postwar era as highway and airline travel became more popular, cross-border rail travel endures — alas, not without political and practical challenges — into the Amtrak and VIA Rail Canada eras.

In this edition of PASSENGER TRAIN ANNUAL we'll look at some of the postwar

ABOVE **Having traded Central Vermont power for Boston & Maine, the southbound** Ambassador **(with two Canadian National cars and a New Haven coach) prepares to depart White River Junction, Vt., in 1963.**
CARL V. EHRKE; CNR HISTORICAL ASSOCIATION COLLECTION.
UPPER INSET: CARL V. EHRKE; CNRHA COLLECTION
MIDDLE AND BOTTOM INSETS: MIKE SCHAFER

ABOVE In a late-1940s view at Vanceboro, Maine, the eastbound *Gull* (left) makes its station stop. On the opposite side of the Maine Central station building is MEC Train 92, awaiting its departure for Bangor. MAINE CENTRAL; GEOFFREY H. DOUGHTY COLLECTION

LEFT CPR class G3 4-6-2 engine 2332 departs Fredericton Junction, N.B. (halfway between the CPR division point of McAdam, N.B., and Saint John), with the eastbound *Gull*. On this 1952 trip the train includes two stainless-steel coaches (Maine Central and/or Boston & Maine). The first car is a B&M baggage-express rebuilt from a former Pullman. KENNETH S. MACDONALD; GORDON D. JOMINI COLLECTION

BELOW Maine Central E7A 711 leads the *Gull* at Fredericton Junction in a June 30, 1956, view. By this time, the E-unit wears MEC's green livery, adopted after joint management with Boston & Maine ended in 1955. Behind the three heavyweight Pullmans is a B&M stainless-steel 6-4-6 sleeper. KENNETH S. MACDONALD; GORDON D. JOMINI COLLECTION

passenger trains that have crossed the international border to serve endpoints in the eastern U.S. and Canada. Their western counterparts — fewer but no less interesting — will be surveyed in a subsequent edition.

Boston to Halifax

The easternmost Canadian endpoint served by cross-border through service was Halifax, the capital city of Nova Scotia and a community with strong economic and social ties to coastal New England and, in particular, to Boston.

The best-known rail passenger service linking these two cities was provided by the *Gull*, which was more of an amalgam of through cars to varied intermediate points than it was a through train. In the course of their overnight trek, the *Gull*'s cars, depending on their endpoints, were handled by Boston & Maine (Boston–Portland, Me.), Maine Central (Portland–Vanceboro, Me.), Canadian Pacific (Vanceboro–Saint John, N.B.), and Canadian National (Saint John–Halifax, N.S.). Until the early 1950s, the longest haul — 732 miles and roughly 23 hours between Boston and Halifax — was reserved for a single through 10-1-2 Pullman heavyweight car; thereafter, the farthest one could travel in a through car — either coach or sleeper — on the *Gull* was the 454 miles between Boston and Saint John.

The *Gull*'s Boston–Saint John Pullman line received lightweight 6-4-6 sleepers in 1955. Boston & Maine's April 24, 1955, consist book gives a detailed look at the normal makeup of the train. On its daily-except-Saturday departures from Boston, the *Gull* carried a Boston–Portland storage mail-express car; a Boston–Eastport (Me.) express car; one Boston–Bangor B&M RPO (30-foot postal apartment), except Sunday; a Boston–Bangor storage mail car; a Boston–Saint John CPR baggage car; a Boston–Bangor coach, Fridays and Sundays only (B&M "American Flyer" on Fridays and MEC heavyweight on Sundays); two Boston–Saint John MEC stainless-steel coaches; the Boston–Saint John B&M *Beach*-series 6-4-6 sleeper; a Boston–Calais (Me.) 10-1-2 heavyweight Pullman (Sundays, Tuesdays, and Thursday only; on Mondays, Wednesdays, and Fridays this car terminated at Bangor); and a Boston–Van Buren (Me.) Bangor & Aroostook 6-4-6 lightweight sleeper.

The *Gull*'s heavy mail and express business ensured its survival through the 1950s, but the train was dismembered after mid-1959. By that time, the *Gull* had the distinction of being the last conventionally equipped train serving Boston's North Station, where its locomotive-hauled cars stood out in a landscape of Budd Rail Diesel Cars.

B&M replaced the Boston–Portland leg of the *Gull* with RDCs on July 12, 1959. The train was thus reduced to a Portland–Saint John schedule until it was discontinued east of Vanceboro by CP on October 25, 1959.

Montreal to the Maritimes via Maine

Opened in 1889, Canadian Pacific's International of Maine Division was a cross-border link between Montreal and the ice-free Atlantic port of Saint John, N.B., that cut across the northern reaches of the State of Maine. In the postwar period, the 482-mile route (which included CP trackage rights over Maine Central between Mattawamkeag and the border town of Vanceboro) was served by a pair of overnight schedules until September 25, 1955. When CP trains 39 and 40 were discontinued east of Megantic, Que., the route's other schedule, operating as previously unnamed trains 40 and 41, became the *Atlantic Limited* at that time.

For passengers needing to travel beyond Saint John to and from Halifax and other points in Nova Scotia, CP offered passage across the Bay of Fundy aboard its long-serving ferry *Princess Helene* (replaced in 1963 by *Princess of Acadia*), with connections on the pier at Digby, N.S., to subsidiary Dominion Atlantic Railway's trains to Halifax. These DAR passenger connections were steam-powered until a pair of Budd RDC "Dayliners" — complete with Dominion Atlantic lettering — arrived in 1956.

Prior to 1949, passenger equipment on the Montreal–Saint John route had been all heavyweight, with the steam-powered trains typically pulled by a 4-6-2 Pacific from CP's G2 or G3 classes. Diesel power was the norm after 1954, with FP7A and FPA-2 cab units most common. In 1970, CP's trio of E8As (more on which later) became fixtures on the *Atlantic Limited*.

When stainless-steel cars began to arrive from Budd in 1954, in anticipation of the April 1955 launch of *The Canadian* (CP's Montreal/Toronto–Vancouver domeliner), many, including "Skyline" and *Park*-series domes, found temporary work on the *Atlantic Limited*.

BELOW **A vestige of New England–Halifax through passenger-train service survived the *Gull's* October 1959 demise east of Vanceboro. In this September 27, 1963, view at Moncton, N.B., a Maine Central baggage-express car loaded with U.S. Mail (one of four cars acquired from Bangor & Aroostook in 1961 as part of MEC's Mail Merchandise Train initiative, which ended three days after this view) is being coupled to CN RS-18 3643 and steam-generator unit 15419 prior to departure for Halifax.** CARL V. EHRKE; CNR HISTORICAL ASSOCIATION COLLECTION

ABOVE The *Atlantic Limited* arrives at Montreal's Windsor Station in June 1969. The first car is a former heavyweight sleeping car, retaining its original six-wheel trucks, converted as a flatcar to carry four 20-foot containers. The rest of the train is a mix of CP's distinctive smooth-sided cars, a Budd "Skyline" dome, and a pair of modernized heavyweight sleepers. One is painted to match CP's stainless-steel fleet, along with the smooth-sided *Grove*-series 10 roomette-5 bedroom sleeper ahead of it. CARL V. EHRKE; CNR HISTORICAL ASSOCIATION COLLECTION

MIDDLE Painted in CP's 1968-vintage "Multimark" image, E8A 1800 has just been uncoupled from the recently arrived *Atlantic Limited* in this June 1975 view at Montreal. KEVIN EuDALY COLLECTION

BOTTOM Recently renamed and re-equipped with former CN cars and locomotives (here, an FPA-4 and F9B), VIA Rail Canada's eastbound *Atlantic* pauses at Saint John, N.B., before continuing to Halifax in May 1980. KEVIN J. HOLLAND

Sleeping cars serving the train's endpoints were augmented in the late 1950s by a Montreal–McAdam, N.B., sleeper and a summer-only sleeper running between Montreal and the Bay of Fundy resort town of St. Andrews, N.B., where one of CP's chain of hotels — the Algonquin — just happened to be located. Both of these cars had been discontinued by 1960.

Following their limited use on the *Atlantic Limited* in 1954-55, dome cars returned in October 1961 when two Skyline dome-coffee shop-coaches were reconfigured to provide dining-room seating instead of coach seats (a change VIA Rail Canada would make permanent in the 1980s). The cars were restored to their coach configuration each summer through 1967 for assignment elsewhere. After that, they were assigned permanently to the *Atlantic Limited*. To avoid having to turn them in Saint John, in the 1970s the two Skyline cars normally assigned to the train (CP 505 and 515) also had their fixed dome seating replaced with walkover seats.

Although modernized heavyweight sleepers were assigned to the train until 1970, two more types of Budd stainless-steel equipment — both of them observation cars — were assigned to the *Atlantic Limited* in the late 1960s. Winding down its secondary transcontinental schedule, *The Dominion*, CP had sufficient *Park*-series sleeper-dome-lounge-observation cars to assign one to each summer run of the *Atlantic Limited* in 1966 and 1968. Their place at the end of the train was taken in the summer of 1967 — Canada's centennial year — by former New York Central *Brook*-series sleeper-lounge-observation cars purchased by CP in 1959 and renamed in the *View* series.

By 1967, the *Atlantic Limited* had become the last intercity passenger train operating in northern New England. It persisted as a CP operation until October 1978, and was fully taken over by VIA Rail Canada on April 1, 1979.

Former CP E- and F-units continued to lead the daily VIA train across the international border, but by the end of 1979 the train had been renamed as VIA's *Atlantic*, its Montreal terminus shifted from CP's Windsor Station to CN's Central Station, its ex-CP cars replaced with former CN equipment, and its operation extended east of Saint John over CN's main line to Halifax. The train's motive-power notoriety continued into this period, with ex-CN FPA-4 and FPB-4 diesels drawing the assignment, complete with FRA-mandated projectile-resistant glazing.

Each trip across Maine entailed *two* crossings of the international boundary, with U.S. Customs formalities handled at Jackman and Vanceboro. For many years, extending into the VIA era, sleeping-car passengers traveling between Canadian endpoints were allowed to sleep through the border inspection.

As something of a political football in Canada, VIA's *Atlantic* was discontinued in 1981, restored in 1985, and discontinued permanently in 1994.

In addition to the *Atlantic Limited*, CP operated a mixed train making a daily-except-Sunday cross-border round-trip between Megantic, Que., and Brownville Junction, Me. Known widely but unofficially as the "Scoot," this relatively obscure train found some celebrity in 1960 when it brought down the curtain on steam-powered passenger trains in New England.

Boston to Montreal via CP and B&M

In direct competition with Canadian National/Central Vermont, Canadian Pacific catered to Montreal–Boston passengers with two daily trains in the postwar years.

The *Alouette* ran on a daytime schedule with the *Red Wing* as its overnight counterpart. The *Alouette*'s signa-

ABOVE In a circa 1950 view, Boston & Maine E7A 3807 leads the jointly operated *Alouette* out of Canadian Pacific's Windsor Station at the start of its daily Montreal–Boston journey. CANADIAN PACIFIC; KEVIN J. HOLLAND COLLECTION

BELOW At Adirondack Jct., Que., with one of CP's three E8s in charge, the Boston-bound *Alouette* has just crossed the St. Lawrence River following the train's departure from Montreal on July 1, 1952. AL PATERSON COLLECTION

passenger train annual 2021 **31**

ABOVE AND RIGHT CP RDCs bring up the rear of a conventional B&M train along the Connecticut River near Norwich, Vt., en route to Wells River, Vt., where they will be cut off to continue their run to Montreal via St. Johnsbury and Newport, Vt., on June 27, 1957. The conventional B&M train will then head east from Wells River to Berlin, N.H. BOTH, JIM SHAUGHNESSY

ture car during the 1940s and early '50s was an arch-roofed CP heavyweight buffet-parlor-observation with an open-air rear platform and illuminated tail sign, one of the last of its kind in main line operation anywhere in North America.

Until late 1954, the *Alouette* ran via Wells River, Vt., and Woodsville, Plymouth, and Concord, N.H. At that time, the *Alouette* was shifted to the *Red Wing's* route via White River Junction, Vt. In Montreal, both trains used CP's Windsor Station.

In October 1956, the *Alouette* name was dropped when the schedule was re-equipped with Budd Rail Diesel Cars. Using pooled CPR and B&M RDCs, this operation, as trains 31 and 32, lasted until 1965.

After March 24, 1958, Wells River was employed as the meeting point for RDCs already serving Montreal and the B&M RDC-3s newly assigned to Boston–Berlin, N.H., operation. South of Wells River, the cars would couple up and run as a single train to and from Boston. Northbound, the RDCs would separate at Wells River and depart for their respective endpoints.

Through much of the postwar period, the *Red Wing* ran on B&M be-

tween Boston and White River Junction combined with Central Vermont's *New Englander*, with both schedules offering through cars between Boston and Montreal. Prior to World War II, the *Red Wing* also carried a through sleeper two days a week between Boston and Quebec City.

The *Red Wing* was discontinued on October 24, 1959. It had been a coach-and-sleeper-only train following the April 26, 1959, discontinuance of its buffet-lounge car.

The former *Alouette* followed its counterpart into the history books in 1965. B&M withdrew from the partnership effective April 25 of that year, at which time the train was reduced to a Montreal–Wells River service. Just over six months later, on October 30, 1965, that remnant of Boston–Montreal through service was also discontinued.

Until the early 1950s, CP also operated local passenger trains between Newport, Vt., and points in Quebec. CP subsidiary Quebec Central forwarded passengers to and from the provincial capital of Quebec City, while CP itself looked after Montreal traffic.

TOP LEFT **CP class G1s 4-6-2 engine 2210 leads the southbound *Alouette* at St. Johnsbury, Vt., in August 1948.** AL PATERSON COLLECTION

MIDDLE **Following the *Alouette*'s conversion to RDCs in October 1956, B&M RDC-2 6204 paused beside the B&M depot at Wells River, Vt., on October 1, 1963. After April 25, 1965, when B&M left the pool, this is as far south from Montreal as the train went.**

BELOW **With Lake Memphremagog in the distance, B&M RDC-2 6204, running as CP Train 32 to Montreal, loads passengers at Newport, Vt., on October 1, 1963. From Newport, CP's Vermont main line extended 64 miles south to Wells River.** BOTH, CARL V. EHRKE; CNR HISTORICAL ASSOCIATION COLLECTION

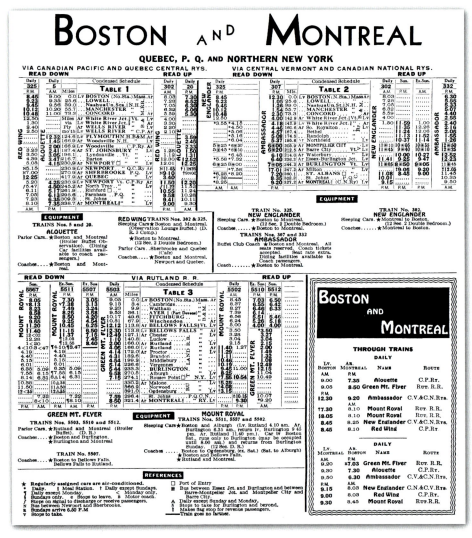

ABOVE **This page from Boston & Maine's September 28, 1941, public timetable summarizes the cross-border offerings of CP, CN, CV, B&M, and Rutland.** KEVIN J. HOLLAND COLLECTION

BELOW **Rutland Railroad leaflet from 1940 promoting its trains to and from Canada.** KEVIN J. HOLLAND COLLECTION

RIGHT **Central Vermont's *Washingtonian* pauses at Essex Jct., Vt., behind CN Class U-1 4-8-4 Northern-type engine 6211 during the train's nightly trek from Montreal to Washington, D.C., over CN, CV, B&M, NH, and PRR rails. The Canadian 4-8-4 will lead the train to White River Junction, Vt., where B&M diesels will take over as far as Springfield, Mass. From New York's Penn Station, PRR GG1 electrics will lead the *Washingtonian* on its final leg.** JIM SHAUGHNESSY

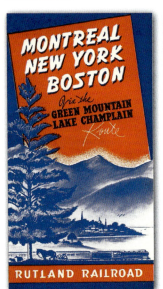

CP's Vermont operations had been among the earliest portions of the vast system to be dieselized, in 1949. Boiler-equipped Alco RS-2s were specified for local passenger train and other duties, while that trio of EMD E-units was ordered as CP's contribution to Montreal–Boston through service with B&M.

These first — and only — E-units purchased new by a Canadian railway were chosen for compatibility with B&M's existing fleet of E7As. Having initially specified E7s, the CP order was changed to E8s when that new model became available. One of the CP E-units initially was intended to handle the Montreal–Newport, Vt., local trains; another was assigned to lead the *Alouette* every second day over its entire Montreal–Boston route, alternating with a B&M unit for mileage equalization. The third CP E-unit was originally assigned to the *Red Wing* between Montreal and Wells River.

New York to Montreal via Rutland

New York City and Montreal were connected by through trains operated by Rutland Railroad (Rail*way* after 1950), in partnership with New York Central and Canadian National. Boston cars were interchanged with B&M at Bellows Falls, Vt., connecting with the

New York–Montreal train at Rutland's namesake Vermont hometown.

The *Mount Royal* was an overnight schedule, leaving Grand Central Terminal after dinner and arriving in Montreal in time for the next business day.

The *Green Mountain Flyer* (in its last years, known simply as the *Green Mountain*) was the Rutland's through day train, with northbound coaches and parlor cars from Boston (via B&M at Bellows Falls) and New York City (via NYC at Troy, N.Y.) merging at Rutland, Vt., before skirting the Green Mountains and leapfrogging across Lake Champlain on the way to the CN connection at Rouses Point, N.Y.

Alas, Rutland Railway was never much of a passenger operator, and it became a freight-only property as the result of a strike in 1953.

Grand Trunk Railway to Portland

Passenger trains were never plentiful on this historic Canadian National system appendage, either, with a daytime coach schedule (unnamed trains 16 and 17) sufficing on the 296-mile Montreal–Portland, Me., route through much of the postwar era. Local CN traffic between Montreal and the Grand Trunk division point of Island Pond, Vt., was served by daytime local trains 11 and 12. On the head end, the improbable sight of a car lettered both "Canadian National" and "U.S. Mail Railway Post Office" only served to reinforce the stature of this Grand Trunk line as North America's first international railroad.

Tourists venturing from Quebec to the Maine beaches were an important source of summer traffic for Grand Trunk. Prior to World War II, an overnight train offered after-dinner departures and pre-breakfast arrivals at both Portland and Montreal. The *Maine Coast Special* operated only in conjunction with the Dominion Day (July 1), Fourth of July, and Labor Day holiday weekends.

So persistent was the tourist market that for six years after trains 16 and 17 were discontinued in September 1960, summer-weekend-only passenger trains operated between Montreal and Portland. Passengers rode in a variety of streamlined CN coaches, while heavyweight parlors and buffet-parlors catered to the first class trade.

Typical steam power came in the form of Canadian National Class J-7 Pacifics and U-1 Mountains. Steam was in regular passenger service east of Island Pond until June 15, 1956, replaced by five Grand Trunk-lettered, steam-generator-equipped GP9s, Nos. 4902-4906. CN diesel power — FP9A and FPA-4 cab units and RS-18 road switchers — also made it to Portland on occasion, particularly during the 1961-1966 summer-only operations. Between late 1957 and early 1959, CN Budd RDC equipment operated locally on the Montreal–Island Pond segment of the route, but did not run through to Portland.

CN's Vermont Connection

Not too far west of the Grand Trunk route, Canadian National's other New England subsidiary was Central Vermont Railway (CV), which linked its parent at Rouses Point, N.Y., with tidewater at New London, Conn., via St. Albans and White River Junction, Vt.

Inaugurated on June 15, 1924, the southbound *Washingtonian* and its northbound running mate, the *Montrealer*, connected their namesake cities by way of an overnight CN-CV-B&M-NH-PRR routing that also served Springfield, Mass., Hartford, Conn., and New York's Pennsylvania Station.

In the days before convenient air travel, the *Montrealer* and *Washingtonian* were patronized by U.S. and Canadian diplomats shuttling between their respective national capitals — Ottawa being just a short connecting trip away from Montreal, while Washington Union Station is within sight of Capitol Hill.

CN's prewar and postwar streamlined coaches could be seen in Boston, New York City, Washington, and intermediate points, with postwar CN 6-4-6 lightweight *Green*-series sleeping cars (leased to the Pullman Company for international operation and sub-lettered accordingly) serving in the *Washingtonian/Montrealer* pool. Conversely, NH, PRR, and B&M lightweight sleeping cars were postwar visitors to CN's Central Station in Montreal. In 1956, for example, NH *Monument Beach* and CN *Greenmount*, both 6-4-6 sleepers, covered one of these Montreal–New York Pullman lines, while a pair of CN cars, *Greenvale* and *Green Lane*, covered the other. NH cars *Popponasett Beach* and *Sound Beach* held down the train's St. Albans–New York Pullman line at the time. Even at this late date, Montreal–Washington service was provided by heavyweight Pullmans; 6 bedroom-lounge cars *Dover Cliffs* and *Dover Straits*, and 8 section-5 bedroom sleepers *Clover Glen* and *Clover Trail*. After 1960, NH lightweight sleeper-lounges *Nutmeg State* and *Pine Tree State* were regularly assigned to the *Washingtonian/Montrealer*.

The CN/CV daytime Boston–Montreal train debuted on April 26, 1926, as the *Ambassador*. On the same date, the *New Englander* debuted as an overnight schedule connecting North Station with Montreal.

ABOVE CV 4-8-2 engine 603 has the southbound *Ambassador* in tow at St. Lambert, Que., in May 1950. The electric line at left is CN's interurban subsidiary Montreal & Southern Counties. AL PATERSON COLLECTION

BELOW A CN Pacific leads the *Ambassador* across the CV trestle at East Alburgh, Vt., in June 1955. JIM SHAUGHNESSY

UPPER RIGHT CV dieselized its passenger trains with RS-3 and GP9 units. The engineer of GP9 4923 watches as mail is loaded during the *Ambassador*'s stop at CV's new Essex Jct., Vt., station in March 1966. JIM SHAUGHNESSY

Traveling over B&M, CV, and CN via Manchester, Concord, and White River Junction, the *Ambassador*'s consist originally included heavyweight coaches, a dining car, a parlor car, and a Pullman 25-seat parlor-observation car over its entire run. Lightweight B&M "American Flyer" coaches, and similar semi-streamlined cars owned by CN, appeared in the mid-1930s and remained fixtures for more than two decades.

Until the mid-1950s, Montreal–New York City through cars were dispatched south of White River Junction in the consist of the *Connecticut Yankee*. By that time, B&M handled the CV *Ambassador* and the CP *Alouette* as a combined train between White River Junction and Boston. B&M's April 1955 consist book specified these cars for a "normal" *Alouette/Ambassador* running from White River Junction to Boston: a Montreal–Boston CN RPO (30-foot postal apartment), except Sunday;

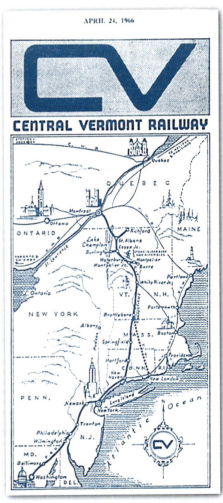

LEFT **B&M F7A 4228 and a B-unit have just brought the northbound *Ambassador* into White River Junction on October 1, 1963. In a few minutes, these two locomotives will be uncoupled and a CV GP9 will take over for the rest of the trip to Montreal. In the distance at right, another pair of B&M F-units can be seen ready to lead the southbound *Ambassador* to Boston.** CARL V. EHRKE; CNR HISTORICAL ASSOCIATION COLLECTION. TIMETABLE, KEVIN J. HOLLAND COLLECTION

ABOVE Amtrak's southbound *Montrealer* in the wee hours at White River Junction, Vt., in the summer of 1974, not long after the train's name had been changed to the *Montrealer* in both directions. MIKE SCHAFER

LEFT Passengers alight from Amtrak's northbound *Montrealer* at Montpelier Jct., Vt., in June 1981. MIKE SCHAFER; BROCHURE AND MENU, KEVIN J. HOLLAND COLLECTION

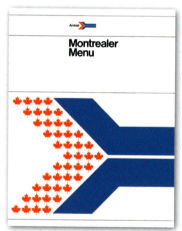

a Montreal–Boston express car (CV or B&M on alternate days); a Montreal–White River CP RPO, except Sunday; a Montreal–Boston combine; a Montreal–Boston "American Flyer" B&M coach; a Montreal–Boston buffet-parlor (B&M or CP on alternate days); a Montreal–Boston CN coach; a White River–Boston coach/smoker, Sunday only; and two Plymouth cars picked up at Concord, N.H.

After 1956, as B&M sought to rid itself of conventional locomotive-hauled passenger trains, the dwindling Boston service was handled by B&M Budd RDCs via a cross-platform connection at White River Junction. The *Ambassador* name was used instead to denote only the Montreal–New York service, which lost its Montreal–White River cafe-grill car in January 1958 and thereafter carried only coaches.

B&M RDCs were assigned sporadically to the *Ambassador*, typically in off-peak months, beginning in January 1959 until April 1961, running through between Springfield, Mass., and Montreal via CV north of White River Junction. Under this operation, a change of trains was required at Springfield for passengers traveling to or from New York City. Despite being an established user of RDCs, CN did not contribute equipment to the *Ambassador* during its periods of RDC operation. CN RDCs did see limited use, however, in local service between Montreal and Island Pond, Vt., from October 1957 until April 1959.

The *Ambassador* and *Montrealer/Washingtonian* (along with CP's *Atlantic Limited*) had survived to become the last privately operated long-distance passenger trains serving northern New England. September 3–4, 1966, marked the practical end of this era as the *Ambassador*, *Montrealer*, and *Washingtonian* all made their final runs.

Six years passed before cross-border service resumed between Montreal and New England, in the form of Amtrak's reincarnation of the *Montrealer/Washingtonian*. This operation debuted with much fanfare on September 30, 1972, and the train name became the *Montrealer* in both directions in May 1974. Except for a suspension between April 1987 and July 1989, service persisted (with some route adjustments) until March 31, 1995, when operation north of St. Albans, Vt., was terminated and, on a new daylight schedule, the train became the *Vermonter*.

Pending final regulatory approval in both the U.S. and Canada, and provision of secure U.S. Customs pre-clearance facilities at Montreal's Central Station, the years-long goal of extending *Vermonter* service north across the border may yet be realized.

Delaware & Hudson

Running north from Albany and following the western shore of Lake Champlain toward the Canadian border, D&H — the aptly named "Bridge Line Route" — was the middle link in passenger service provided by New York Central/Penn Central and Canadian Pacific between New York City and Montreal. Operating over subsidiary Napierville Junction Railway north of Rouses Point, N.Y., and across the international boundary, D&H employed trackage rights over CP between Delson, Que., and Montreal's Windsor Station.

Debuting in 1923, the *Laurentian* offered travelers a daylight schedule in both directions between its endpoint cities. Semi-streamlined cars entered service in the 1930s and, up front, Alco RS-2 diesels (and a solitary boiler-equipped RS-3) took over from steam in 1953.

In 1967, D&H President F.C. "Buck" Dumaine, Jr., challenged the declining passenger market when he acquired a group of stainless-sheathed passenger cars from Denver & Rio Grande Western, and a quartet of Alco PA-1 diesels from Santa Fe, to re-equip the *Laurentian*. The reinvented train's time in the spotlight was brief, however, as service expired on April 30, 1971.

The *Laurentian*'s running mate was the overnight *Montreal Limited*, linking Montreal and New York City with through coaches and sleeping cars.

A little more than three years after D&H ended its passenger service to Montreal, those blue-and-gray PAs and passenger cars returned to Windsor Station with the August 6, 1974, inauguration of Amtrak's *Adirondack*. This

BELOW **Delaware & Hudson's northbound** *Montreal Limited* **arrives at Montreal West, Que., on March 7, 1969, behind RS-2 4005. The previous year's Penn Central merger is reflected in the train's three sleeping cars, with two still wearing New York Central markings and one in Pennsylvania Railroad paint.** KEVIN EuDALY COLLECTION

ABOVE **D&H** *Willsboro Point*, at Colonie, N.Y., in October 1974, was one of two CP Skyline domes leased, renamed, and repainted for use on the *Adirondack*. ROLF H. SCHNEIDER; KEVIN J. HOLLAND COLLECTION

LEFT The southbound *Laurentian* calls at Port Henry, N.Y., in April 1965. This was D&H's day train between Albany and Montreal, and was the running mate of the overnight *Montreal Limited*. Ex-Santa Fe PA-1s replaced RS units in 1967. KEVIN J. HOLLAND COLLECTION

BELOW D&H PA-1 19 rests at Montreal with the *Adirondack* in September 1975. The train includes two cars each from D&H and Amtrak, but lacks a dome. KEVIN EuDALY COLLECTION

Montreal–New York City daytime train was a then-unique hybrid, funded by Amtrak and New York State's Department of Transportation and initially employing refurbished D&H equipment.

D&H even leased a pair of CP Skyline coach-buffet-dome cars, complete with D&H names (*Willsboro Point* and *Bluff Point*), numbers (35 and 36), and yellow striping, for service north of Albany–Rensselaer until the spring of 1975. Domes from Amtrak's own fleet were then assigned, before Turboliner equipment (in early 1977) and later Amfleet took over. Remarkably, the *Adirondack* regained its domeliner status from 2007 through 2018, when Amtrak's last dome car, *Ocean View* (a full-length Budd dome built in 1955 for the *Empire Builder* and retained by Amtrak for special service), was assigned north of Albany–Rensselaer on select days during the peak fall-foliage season. Ex-CP

ABOVE **Passengers disembarking from a recently arrived CP Rail suburban Town Train look over the inaugural run of the *Adirondack* at Windsor Station on August 6, 1974.** KEVIN J. HOLLAND COLLECTION

BELOW **Amtrak Turboliners replaced the *Adirondack*'s Delaware & Hudson equipment in early 1977. On June 1, 1979, a Turboliner and the ex-CP cars of VIA's recently arrived *Atlantic Limited* occupy the open-air platform tracks just beyond Windsor Station's truncated train shed.** GEORGE H. DRURY

passenger train annual 2021 **41**

domes returned to the *Adirondack* for a few weeks in 2012, in the immediate aftermath of Hurricane Sandy, when VIA Rail Canada provided Amtrak with two sets of Budd cars, including *Park*-series dome observations, to allow the train's usual Amfleet cars to be redeployed.

In 1986, as part of the consolidation of VIA Rail Canada's Montreal station operations, the *Adirondack's* Canadian terminus was shifted from Windsor Station to Central Station, requiring a reroute over CN between Montreal and Rouses Point.

With the unprecedented closure of the U.S.-Canada land border to nonessential traffic due to the coronavirus pandemic, operation of the *Adirondack* was suspended north of Albany–Rensselaer in March 2020. Service is expected to resume when the border fully reopens.

From the Northeast to Toronto

To a varying extent, New York Central, Pennsylvania Railroad, and Lehigh Valley all offered postwar through and connecting service between New York City and Toronto via Buffalo.

Lehigh Valley's contribution was the first to go, when the railroad discontinued all passenger service in February 1962. Until then, the jointly operated *Maple Leaf* offered a colorful mix of cars from LV, PRR, Pullman, and CN.

NYC and successor Penn Central's cross-border passenger trains were operated between Buffalo and Toronto under an arrangement with Canadian Pacific that took effect in 1897, with the two roads' jointly owned Toronto, Hamilton & Buffalo Railway serving as intermediary — "Connecting the Two Great Systems," as TH&B advertised on its postwar public timetables.

NYC's participation in the TH&B/CP pool created a broad range of options for sleeping-car passengers travelling between Toronto and points in the Northeastern U.S. Lightweight sleeping cars were operated daily through the 1950s via the NYC/TH&B/CP pool between Toronto and New York, Boston, Pittsburgh and Cleveland. By October 1963 Cleveland and Pittsburgh had been dropped as through-car destinations. Between October 1964 and the introduction of Toronto–Buffalo RDCs in October 1970, a streamlined 10-6 between New York City and Toronto endured as the last through sleeper option on this once-important network.

Varied consists were typical of the Toronto–Buffalo pool service until the RDCs took over. Heavyweight equipment from all three partners mingled with lightweight cars owned by NYC and Canadian Pacific. In the 1950s TH&B contemplated purchasing a group of NYC smooth-sided streamlined coaches to modernize its part of this service, but did not pursue the idea beyond some initial correspondence.

ABOVE One of two NYC 4-6-4 Hudson engines sold to subsidiary Toronto, Hamilton & Buffalo accelerates from Toronto's suburban Sunnyside station toward downtown with Buffalo–Toronto Train 722 on December 16, 1953. TH&B Hudson 501 had been NYC 5311. DICK GEORGE; KEVIN J. HOLLAND COLLECTION

BELOW Lehigh Valley PA1s are in charge of the *Maple Leaf* at NK Tower in Newark, N.J., inbound to Pennsylvania Station from Toronto on November 22, 1958. The first three cars wear LV colors, followed by a pair of heavyweight Pullmans and three lightweight Canadian National cars. WALT GROSSELFINGER; KEVIN EuDALY COLLECTION

ABOVE CP RS-18 8780 and RS-10 8481 lead Train 322, the *Ontarian*, on CN at Toronto's Sunnyside station on July 2, 1966. This was a jointly operated NYC-TH&B-CP Buffalo–Toronto train. CP RDCs took over in 1970. ROGER PUTA

BELOW In the same train, TH&B coach 75 bears lettering for the three Toronto–Buffalo pool partners. ROGER PUTA

RIGHT Inaugurated in April 1981 and operated by VIA Rail Canada over its Canadian mileage, Amtrak's *Maple Leaf* passes Bayview Junction, Ont., on its way to Toronto from New York City in May 2007. KEVIN J. HOLLAND

The locomotive pool on these jointly operated trains provided an opportunity for NYC's handsome 4-6-4 Hudson engines to run their final Canadian miles, after they were bumped from Detroit–Buffalo runs by dieselization of that route's passenger trains on June 16, 1953. (See "Canada Southern" section below.) The reprieve ended on March 22, 1954, when NYC and TH&B dieselized their portions of the Toronto–Buffalo pool.

After the Buffalo–Hamilton segment was dieselized, boiler-equipped NYC GP7s, GP9s, and RS-3s were frequent visitors to Hamilton's Hunter Street Station. There they were relieved by CP or TH&B locomotives for the trip (using trackage rights) across Canadian National's Oakville Subdivision to Toronto. Conversely, TH&B's three passenger-service GP9s often ran over the Welland–Buffalo portion of NYC's Canada Division and into Buffalo Central Terminal. CPR diesels lacked the necessary Automatic Train Control (ATC) hardware to operate over NYC beyond Welland, although between 1931 and 1954 a total of nine CP Pacifics had ATC fitted at various times and regularly ran all the way into Buffalo.

Those CP RDCs continued to connect Toronto with Buffalo into the VIA era until April 1981, when a new Amtrak/VIA New York City–Toronto train, the *Maple Leaf*, was inaugurated. The new train, an extension of an existing Amtrak Empire Service schedule, employed Amtrak equipment over its entire run, but was operated by VIA crews over its Canadian mileage between the border crossing at Niagara Falls and Toronto Union Station. In Canada, the *Maple Leaf* used CN's main line between the border and Hamilton, Ont., rather than the previous (former TH&B) routing.

A New York City–Toronto sleeping car returned, briefly and only on weekends, when Amtrak introduced a new *Niagara Rainbow* between early 1994 and September 1995, in addition to the *Maple Leaf*'s existing daytime schedule.

As with the *Adirondack*, the *Maple Leaf*'s border crossing was suspended during the coronavirus pandemic.

Canada Southern: Detroit–Buffalo

Largely forgotten today, until the 1970s New York Central and successor Penn Central maintained a once-important main line route between Detroit and Buffalo, with members of NYC's "Great Steel Fleet" of passenger trains running north of Lake Erie through the mostly rural farmlands of southern Ontario. On December 31, 1882, Michigan Central Railroad acquired Canada Southern Railway (CASO) under a 21-year lease, and on January 1, 1904, MC consolidated its lease for 999 years. In August 1929, MC in turn sub-leased CASO to parent New York Central (becoming NYC's Canada Division), before MC itself disappeared as an independent property with its February 1930 merger into NYC. It was an alphabet soup that kept the lawyers busy, but also gave NYC a time-competitive alternate route for its Midwest–East Coast passenger and freight traffic.

This cross-border "air line" had been made even more efficient in 1910 with the completion of MC's Detroit River Tunnel (DRT), which dispensed with slow car ferries. From the tunnel's official opening on July 26, 1910, trains were pulled through by electric locomotives drawing current from a third rail.

By the end of World War II, the route between Detroit and Buffalo was an important link in NYC's broader traffic between the eastern seaboard and the Midwest, carrying both freight and some of the company's most celebrated streamliners.

A prominent member of the Great Steel Fleet, NYC's streamlined *Empire State Express* had an auspicious debut, making its first runs on December 7, 1941. The daytime train's Budd stainless-steel cars operated between Grand Central Terminal and Cleveland Union Terminal, with a separate Detroit sec-

ABOVE **The inaugural run of Amtrak's *Niagara Rainbow* was photographed at Utica, N.Y., en route from New York City to Detroit via Buffalo and southern Ontario on October 30, 1974.** JOHN BARTLEY; KEVIN EuDALY COLLECTION

BELOW **Two decades earlier, New York Central 4-6-4 Hudson engine 5363 departs St. Thomas, Ont., with the Detroit–Buffalo section of the *Empire State Express* on August 27, 1951. Just shy of its tenth birthday, the train is no longer a stainless-steel streamliner. It will head east over NYC's Canada Division (the former Canada Southern) to Fort Erie, Ont., before returning to U.S. soil at Buffalo, where its through cars will be combined with the Cleveland section for forwarding to New York City.** JOHN F. HUMISTON; KEVIN J. HOLLAND COLLECTION

tion splitting at Buffalo and running over NYC's Canada Division. The *Empire State Express* thus beat *The Canadian* (also built by Budd, for CP) as the first stainless-steel train in regular Canadian service by 12½ years.

By mid-1953, NYC Train 358, the combined *Canadian-Niagara*, was one of five daily eastbound passenger trains between Detroit and Buffalo, and was the only one of the quintet to operate between Welland and Buffalo via Niagara Falls, crossing the international border at Suspension Bridge. The other eastbound Canada Division trains of NYC's celebrated "Great Steel Fleet" followed the more direct route between Welland and Buffalo via the International Bridge linking Fort Erie, Ont., and Buffalo.

Between Chicago's Central Station and Detroit, the *Canadian-Niagara* of 1953 carried through cars destined for Toronto and Buffalo. Upon arrival in Detroit, the train was broken up, and the Toronto-bound cars (coaches and two sleepers — a heavyweight 12-1 and a lightweight NYC 10-6) departed through the Detroit River Tunnel in the consist of CP Train 20 (which itself was known as the *Canadian* until the April 24, 1955, debut of *The Canadian*, CP's Budd-built domeliner). The "Niagara" portion of NYC Train 358 continued on with its Chicago–Buffalo coaches, 8-section Pullman buffet-lounge, and 10-5 *Cascade*-series sleeper. At Detroit, every night except Saturday, it picked up a 22-roomette sleeper for Buffalo. Although the combined train was effectively split in Detroit, it was referred to as the *Canadian-Niagara* for its entire Chicago-Buffalo run.

NYC's final public timetable, issued on December 3, 1967, still listed two daily passenger trains in each direction (plus a daily-except-Saturday eastbound) between Buffalo and Detroit via southern Ontario, and a handful of through sleeping cars remained. Successor Penn Central dropped the third eastbound schedule on July 15, 1968, maintaining two trains in each direction until November 8, 1970, when all PC Buffalo–Detroit passenger service through Canada was discontinued.

After a four-year absence, Amtrak re-introduced passenger service over the old Canada Southern route on October 30, 1974. Named the *Niagara Rainbow*, the daily round trip between New York City and Detroit was discontinued on January 31, 1979.

Chicago to Toronto and Montreal

Through service on the almost 850-mile route linking these three major cities began in earnest in May 1900 with the debut of the *International Limited*.

ABOVE **As they had done for years on a daily basis, Santa Fe warbonnets and Canadian National maple leaves rubbed shoulders at Chicago's Dearborn Station in October 1964.** JIM BOYD; KEVIN EuDALY COLLECTION

BELOW **Grand Trunk Western GP9 4952 leads the eastbound *International Limited* on parent CN at Dundas, Ont., in April 1967. A connecting bus waits to take passengers to downtown Hamilton, Ont.** KEVIN J. HOLLAND COLLECTION

Prior to Canadian National's creation in the 1920s, Grand Trunk Railway operated the full length of this route. After CN entered the picture, trains were handled by subsidiary Grand Trunk Western (GTW) between Chicago's Dearborn Station and the border at Port Huron, Mich. Parent CN took over on Canadian soil, having employed the historic St. Clair Tunnel to cross the border between Port Huron and Sarnia, Ont. Equipment between Chicago and Montreal was routinely a mix from both roads, as well as cars operated by Pullman (some of which wore CN colors).

Steam on this route lasted well into the late 1950s on both sides of the border, with GP9s dieselizing the GTW mileage and frequently running through as far as Toronto. In the late 1960s, CN GP9s and FP9As operated to Chicago.

Even with parent CN's pro-passenger stance, the late 1960s saw a rapid retrenchment of the route's cross-border trains. Three daily round trips were offered until November 1964, when the eastbound *Inter-City Limited* became a Chicago–Port Huron train. It was discontinued entirely three years later.

When CN and CP ended their three-decade-old Pool Train Agreement for services between Montreal and Toronto in 1965, the *International Limited* effectively became a Toronto–Chicago operation. Five years later, on June 12, 1970, this train also lost its cross-border status (but, oddly, retained its name) when it became a Port Huron–Chicago operation. At that time, the *Maple Leaf* became the sole survivor of the once-impressive CN/GTW cross-border fleet, but Amtrak's arrival on May 1, 1971, ended even that last vestige.

After an absence of more than 11 years, Chicago–Toronto through service was restored when Amtrak and VIA Rail Canada introduced the jointly operated *International Limited* on October 31, 1982. Previously, Amtrak and VIA passengers had to make their own way across the border between Port Huron and Sarnia before resuming their journeys on different trains. The new through train's name was shortened to the *International* in June 1983, and service — with a frequently changing mix of VIA and Amtrak equipment types — lasted until April 23, 2004.

Detroit to Toronto

While CN did its best to maintain through service between these two cities via car ferries and bus connections across the Detroit River, CP's competing trains (as well as those reaching farther west to Chicago in conjunction with NYC) took advantage of the speed and convenience of NYC's Detroit River Tunnel to travel between Detroit's Michigan Central station and Windsor, Ont.

In Detroit, CN trains used subsidiary Grand Trunk Western's small downtown station on Brush Street. On the Canadian side of the river, CN maintained a passenger station near its Windsor ferry slips before relocating to a modern facility in adjacent Walkerville in the early 1960s.

Summing up and looking ahead

Until the global coronavirus pandemic closed the U.S.-Canada land border to non-essential traffic in March 2020, international passenger-rail service was offered between Montreal and New York City (the *Adirondack*); Toronto and New York City (the *Maple Leaf*); and Vancouver and Seattle (the *Cascades*). Canada's border reopened to non-essential (and fully vaccinated) U.S. visitors on August 9, 2021, but resumption of international passenger-train operations must wait until the U.S. government reciprocates with its own border reopening, which had not occurred as this edition of Passenger Train Annual went to press.

We'll continue our "Ties That Bind" coverage in the next edition, heading west and surveying trains reaching north of the border to connect Winnipeg and Vancouver with points in the U.S.

Portions of the preceding text have been excerpted and adapted from the author's Passenger Trains of Northern New England *(TLC, 2004) and* Rails to the Border, Vol. 1 *(BRMNA, 1999); © Kevin J. Holland, All Rights Reserved.*

LEFT With locomotives and cars clad in the new CN system graphics unveiled in 1961, GTW's *Maple Leaf* (not to be confused with the LV/PRR/CN train of that name) departs Chicago in 1969. JIM HEUER; KEVIN EuDALY COLLECTION

ABOVE NYC Class DES-3 electric motor 538 has brought CP Train 21, the *Chicago Express* from Montreal, through the Detroit River Tunnel and into Detroit's Michigan Central Terminal on June 11, 1949. JOHN F. HUMISTON; KEVIN J. HOLLAND COLLECTION

BELOW With a typical mix of Amtrak and VIA equipment, the westbound *International* pauses on CN at London, Ont., in April 1992. The VIA F40PH will lead the train all the way to Chicago. Amtrak Superliners and VIA LRC cars were also assigned to the *International*, as were Amtrak locomotives. JOHN EULL; KEVIN J. HOLLAND COLLECTION

Amtrak's North

Traveling the "alternate route" between Chicago and Seattle in May 1972

Viewed from the Dutch door of a former Great Northern dome coach, Amtrak's westbound *North Coast Hiawatha* includes cars of Northern Pacific, SP&S, and GN heritage. Arguably, perhaps, there is more impressive scenery along the former NP route than on rival GN's route through Montana. Here, the *NCH* skirts the Jefferson River between Livingston and Butte, Mont., in May 1972. MIKE SCHAFER

Coast Hiawatha

BY MIKE SCHAFER

ABOVE Amtrak representative/host Linn Sinclair was aboard our *North Coast Hiawatha* in May 1972. At the time, the infant Amtrak often provided hosts for its long-distance trains.

BELOW Fellow traveler Harold Edmonson (right) confers with the crew on The Milwaukee Road's station platform at La Crosse, Wis.

RIGHT Passenger representative Linn Sinclair and the westbound *North Coast Hiawatha* during its stop at La Crosse. Ex-Chicago, Burlington & Quincy Vista-Dome parlor-observation car *Silver Veranda* trailed our colorful train, providing first class daytime service. The car went only as far as Minneapolis, where it was detached from the train, turned, and sent back east on the next Chicago-bound *North Coast Hiawatha*. THREE PHOTOS, MIKE SCHAFER; BROCHURE, AUTHOR'S COLLECTION

Over the first 50 years of Amtrak's existence, a surprising number of notable, long-distance trains have come and gone — "late and lamented" if you will. But few have been as late and lamented as Amtrak's Chicago–Seattle *North Coast Hiawatha*, which operated from 1971 until 1979. May it rust in peace.

What became the *North Coast Hiawatha* began in the early days of Amtrak as a nameless triweekly train between Minneapolis and Spokane, Wash., via Butte, Mont., added to the Amtrak schedules that went into effect on May 1, 1971. Before Amtrak was launched, planners struggled with choosing which of several route options would be ideal for a single train that would link the Chicago and Seattle endpoints, finally settling on Milwaukee Road (Chicago–Minneapolis), Burlington Northern's ex-Great Northern main line (Minneapolis–Spokane), and BN's ex-Northern Pacific main line (Spokane–Seattle). A majority of the route—Minneapolis–Spokane—was that of the pre-Amtrak *Empire Builder*, which had used BN's ex-Chicago, Burlington & Quincy between Chicago and St. Paul, thence BN's ex-GN across the northern tier via Fargo, N. Dak., Havre, Mont., Glacier National Park, and Seattle, Wash.

It turns out that Senator Mike Mansfield (home: Butte, Mont.) was miffed that Butte, the largest city in the state, was bypassed by the Amtrak version of preferred Chicago–Seattle service via Glacier National Park. So, under the provision of the Amtrak act that prompted the new carrier to launch at least two experimental routes per year, Amtrak inaugurated a nameless, triweekly train between Minneapolis and Spokane, Wash., that operated over BN's ex-NP main line between the Twin Cities and Seattle via St. Cloud, Minn., Bismarck, N.D., and Billings and Butte, Mont.

passenger train annual 2021   51

The success of that endeavor prompted Amtrak to extend the train east to Chicago — and in its own time slot — via The Milwaukee Road (as with the *Builder*) effective with the November 14, 1971, Amtrak timetable—Amtrak's first nationwide timetable done in-house. And, it had been given a name — *North Coast Hiawatha* — by Passenger Train Journal founder Kevin McKinney, who worked for the new carrier during its formative years.

Westbound, the *NCH* left Chicago at noon three times a week, arriving in Spokane late the following day and then being combined with the daily *Empire Builder* — which left Chicago in mid-afternoon. The *Builder* had an overall faster schedule, catching up with the *NCH* at Spokane. There, the two trains were combined for the remainder of the overnight journey to Seattle via BN's former NP main line via Pasco and Yakima, Wash.

TOP LEFT **On-board representative Linn Sinclair greets passengers on the** *North Coast Hiawatha*.

LEFT **Up in the dome, Linn Sinclair discusses rail travel with a passenger aboard our** *NCH* **as the train followed the Mississippi River through Minnesota.**

LOWER LEFT **Linn waves at some fishermen as our** *North Coast Hi* **rolls across the former Great Northern's Stone Arch Bridge spanning the Mississippi River in downtown Minneapolis.**

BELOW **Linn actively patroled her train, making certain her passengers were comfortable and answering their questions. Here she talks with a first class passenger in the Vista-Dome parlor-observation car** *Silver Veranda*.
ALL, MIKE SCHAFER

LEFT Our train is but minutes away from the Minneapolis Great Northern Station as we curve off the Stone Arch Bridge. A pair of Milwaukee Road E-units handled our train between Chicago and Minneapolis. Former GN and Northern Pacific motive power took over from here west.

BELOW Our train at Minneapolis station after our Milwaukee Road E-units were swapped with Burlington Northern power, with two of the units still sporting Northern Pacific livery.

FACING PAGE TOP The second day of our trip put us on BN's ex-Northern Pacific main line—on which we would remain the rest of the trip to Seattle. This morning view from the vestibule of our sleeper revealed that we were getting into some scenic territory in eastern Montana. The signal system on the former NP main still had classic semaphores.

FACING PAGE BOTTOM An extended stop at Billings, Mont., allowed us to stroll about the station grounds while our train was being serviced. ALL, MIKE SCHAFER

Between Chicago and the Twin Cities, the *NCH* had a companion train, the *Twin Cities Hiawatha*, that operated on days when the *North Coast Hiawatha* didn't. As a result, the Chicago–Milwaukee–Minneapolis corridor had double-daily service — a minimum for good corridor operation.

The *NCH* grew to have significant ridership while also providing (arguably) an overall more scenic route. An opportunity to ride nearly the entire route happened in the spring of 1972 when friend and business associate Harold Edmonson and I made a trip to the West Coast. I had ridden portions of The Milwaukee Road between Chicago and Minneapolis, but it was all new west of the Twin Cities for both of us. I really looked forward to this trip—my first transcon train ride—but the day before we left, along came the "wouldn't you know it?!" whammy. I suddenly came down with the nastiest upper-

respiratory plague I ever had since my week in the children's ward in 1957 at Swedish-American Hospital, Rockford, Ill., with asthma, bronchitis, and double pneumonia.

I simply couldn't pass up this trip, especially since Amtrak was sponsoring us as journalists. And so, around noon on May 15, 1972, Harold and a coughing, sneezing, wheezing me boarded an on-time *NCH*.

We had a fascinating, eclectic consist that included an A-B-A set of BN F-units, Santa Fe baggage car, NP baggage car, Spokane, Portland & Seattle coach, *Empire Builder* dome coach, a BN ex-GN coach, a BN diner-lounge, and a *California Zephyr* sleeper. Operating only between Chicago and Minneapolis was former Chicago, Burlington & Quincy Vista-Dome parlor-observation car *Silver Veranda* (which I had photographed wrecked in Lee, Ill., six years earlier; see *PTJ* 2020–4), that provided first class service between Chicago and the Twin Cities. This car would "turn" at the Twin Cities on the next eastbound *NCH*, providing a first class "parlor"-type service that Milwaukee Road had provided with its *Afternoon Hiawatha* on a schedule close to that of Amtrak's new *NCH*.

Aboard our train was an Amtrak representative, Linn Sinclair. Amtrak had hired a raft of such individuals to "host" various trains while addressing the concerns of travelers.

FACING PAGE TOP **During the extended servicing stop at Billings, Mont., passengers were permitted to stroll about the station grounds. The dining-car crew took advantage of the beautiful weather as well.**

FACING PAGE BOTTOM **Built in 1902, the sprawling Livingston, Mont., station once served as the gateway to Yellowstone Park for travelers riding NP. Today, the station has been restored to its former glory and serves as a multipurpose anchor for the downtown historic district of Livingston. During this stop, our motive power was changed out, with BN 9790 and its mates swapped for an A-B-A set of F-units still in NP colors.**

ABOVE **Between Billings and Livingston, our train was sidetracked to meet our counterpart, the eastbound *North Coast Hiawatha*, sporting a former *California Zephyr* sleeper-lounge-observation car.**

BELOW **As we neared Butte, our train climbed up through Homestake Pass, the Continental Divide, providing breathtaking scenery.** ALL, MIKE SCHAFER

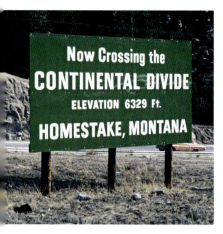

TOP LEFT **The NP line parallels Interstate 90 for much of the route. NP/BN maintained this sign for passengers.**

TOP RIGHT **During the extended Butte stop, we chatted with some BN personnel along with a former GN dining-car attendant. The BN men were making sure the operation of the *North Coast Hiawatha* was going smoothly.**

ABOVE LEFT **This scene at Butte looks like it was taken when Northern Pacific still existed, yet we're in the Burlington Northern/Amtrak era in 1972. We were surprised to see a former NP bus awaiting at the Butte depot, serving (as it did in the good old days) as a connection between Butte and Helena, Mont., the latter being the state capital, which with the coming of Amtrak lost passenger train service (NP/BN's *Mainstreeter* used the Helena route between Logan and Garrison, Mont.).**

ABOVE RIGHT **Butte provided another opportunity for strolling the station platform. I went to the head end to photograph the new power we had received at Livingston. Though the NP livery still looked good, the NP heralds had been removed.**

RIGHT **Our *North Coast Hi* had a nearly two-hour layover at Spokane, Wash., before the *Empire Builder* caught up to it and the two Amtrak trains combined. This allowed time for a night shot or two, plus my taxi ride to an all-night pharmacy to get meds for my upper-respiratory infection.** ALL, MIKE SCHAFER

Up to this point of my life, I had never made a Western transcon trip. Oh, I had ridden Western transcons before, but only locally. On this trip, though, we would ride the *NCH* all the way to Seattle — and along a route that initially had been rejected by the new Amtrak. Indeed, I had only ridden snippets of The Milwaukee Road's popular Chicago–Milwaukee–Twin Cities route: Chicago–Milwaukee, Columbus–Wisconsin Dells, Tomah–New Lisbon. Significant of what I hadn't ridden was the very scenic segment between La Crosse and the Twin Cites, whereby the route skirts the Mississippi River. Fortunately, that stretch was covered before dusk.

At this early time in Amtrak's history, the carrier used the former Great Northern depot in Minneapolis, which had also been used by Northern Pacific and Burlington Route. Milwaukee Road had its own Minneapolis depot, but it was a stub-end facility that required back-up moves for through trains. The depot headhouse remains intact in 2021, serving as part of a new hotel complex.

Once away from Minneapolis, we were on BN's former Northern Pacific rails as far as Spokane, Wash. An uncomfortable night of hacking and coughing kept me awake most of the time, and probably Harold too in the lower bunk. We were assigned to a bedroom in a good old 10-roomette 6-double bedroom sleeper.

Morning light found us in Glendive, Mont., and we looked forward to a day of remarkable scenery — more than I would see in the coming years during the second day of numerous cross-country trips on the *Empire Builder*. Number 9's leisurely schedule allowed for extended platform strolls at principal stops — Billings, Livingston, Butte. The weather was beautiful and the crews friendly. At Livingston, our motive-power set was swapped for another.

Scenerywise, the highlight of the day-long trip across Montana was the approach to Butte. Our train began the climb to Homestake Pass, winding through increasingly rugged mountain terrain. The pinnacle of BN's ex-NP main line at the pass was well-marked. Shortly after, our train curved onto the south face of the mountain, and we were looking down and across a vast

ABOVE **Late during the second night of our trip, during the long station stop at Spokane, Wash., our train was combined with the westbound** *Empire Builder*. **The next morning as we cruised and curved along the Yakima River, still on former NP trackage, we could see our expanded consist, with the** *Empire Builder* **cars forward in the train.** MIKE SCHAFER

FACING PAGE **End of the line. Seattle's King Street Station marked the end of our trip on the** *North Coast Hi*, **but it was not our ultimate destination. A few hours later we would continue to Portland on Amtrak's** *Mount Rainier*. MIKE SCHAFER

valley, with Interstate 90 at the base, so far down that the autos and trucks looked like models. Looking forward toward the horizon at a hazy skyline, we suddenly realized we were looking at Butte. It was a breathtaking highlight of the day's trip across Montana.

Our train quickly descended the face of the mountain range and rolled to a halt at the rambling brick ex-NP depot. I had been here some three years earlier in 1969 to photograph NP's eastbound *North Coast Limited* and Union Pacific's *Butte Special*, and the grounds generally were unchanged. We detrained and yakked with train crews and a couple of passenger department officials. A bus with a roll sign marked "NP North Coast Limited Connection" linked Butte with Helena, the capital of Montana. In due time, we were off again and headed to the former Northern Pacific diner for a splendid supper served on NP dining-car china. Yes, in the early days of Amtrak, one could still enjoy meals on real dining-car china.

West of Butte, the scenery became even more spectacular, and at a number of places we saddled up to The Milwaukee Road's paralleling Twin Cities–Seattle/Tacoma main line, electrified between Harlowton, Mont., and Avery, Idaho, on the north side of our train. Unfortunately, we didn't see any action

on the Milwaukee. At Lombard, Mont., we passed under the Milwaukee as BN's ex-NP main line struck north to Sandpoint, Idaho.

At Sandpoint, our ex-NP main line joined BN's ex-Great Northern main line. Before the 1970 BN merger, GN and NP shared trackage for the nearly 20 miles west to Spokane, Wash.

Arrival at Spokane was about a half hour before midnight. We had a scheduled two-hour-plus layover here as our train waited for the *Empire Builder* to catch up with us. The extended layover gave me a chance to taxi myself to an all-night pharmacy for more medicine for my full-blown sinus/ear infection.

The *Builder* rolled in at 1:20AM, and the combining of the two trains was shortly underway, as was sleep for the next five hours or so. At this time, Amtrak's *Builder* (and *NCH*) operated via BN's ex-NP main line between Spokane and Seattle via Yakima, Wash., which was not the case in later years (and currently) of Amtrak's *Empire Builder* routing.

With a dawn arrival at Yakima, Wash., we still had some 160 scenic miles to go before reaching Seattle's King Street Station. The daylight scenery along the old NP west of Pasco did not disappoint, with stretches of waterside running along the Yakima River. A climb over the Pacific Range brought us down to Puget Sound and King Street Station on the south side of downtown Seattle. We had six hours before our connecting train to Portland — our extended destination for this segment of our circle trip. This gave me time to visit a BN doctor in downtown Seattle (next to Seattle's monorail line, as it turned out) to get some wickedly strong prescriptions for all that ailed me — unfortunately throughout one of the best train rides I ever had that cannot be repeated unless Amtrak ever revives it — which, if you've seen Amtrak's recently released proposed service expansions, may well happen.

Five Decades

62 passenger train **annual** 2021

# of Amtrak
A 50th anniversary photo album

The 1970s saw the melting pot of Amtrak's "rainbow era" evolve into the mechanical uniformity and stability of Amfleet and the Superliners. Although a group of contentious train discontinuances in late 1979 ended Amtrak's first decade on a sour note, the 1980s saw progress with the introduction of *Auto Train*, the *California Zephyr* (the renamed *San Francisco Zephyr*, partially rerouted over Amtrak holdout Denver & Rio Grande Western), and two cross-border trains serving Toronto: the *International* from Chicago and the *Maple Leaf* from New York City. The '90s witnessed expansive state-funded operations in California, North Carolina, Illinois, Missouri, and elsewhere, and saw the stalwart F40PH pass its motive-power torch to GE's Genesis diesel models. Amtrak greeted the new millenium with Acela service on the revitalized Northeast Corridor, and rebranded its national system with a new logo. The first two decades of the 21st century saw more new equipment, culminating in today's Siemens trainsets and the second generation of Acela.

COUNTERCLOCKWISE FROM LEFT
1970s: Melting pot at Chicago in November 1978.
1980s: Turboliner at Milwaukee in July 1980.
1990s: A *San Diegan* at San Diego in 1992.
2000s: Acela Express, February 2003.
2010s: A Siemens Charger at Kansas City in 2019.
DAN POPE, DAVID OROSZI COLLECTION; KEVIN EuDALY COLLECTION; ANDY SMITH; JIM BOYD, KEVIN EuDALY COLLECTION; KEVIN EuDALY COLLECTION

passenger train annual 2021   63

1971-1981

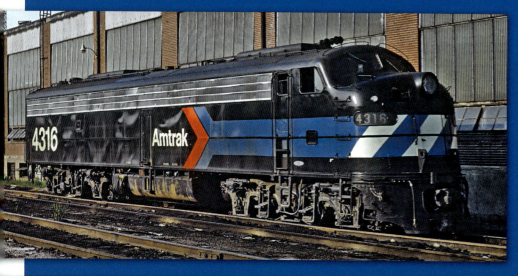

TOP LEFT Former Penn Central E8A 4316 wears its one-of-a-kind Amtrak paint at Chicago. ROGER PUTA

LEFT Former Union Pacific and Burlington Northern E-units move the *San Francisco Zephyr* through suburban Chicago in May 1972. W. SUNKEL; KEVIN EuDALY COLLECTION

TOP INSET E9A 410, at Martinsburg, W. Va., in June 1974, shows off Amtrak's first official diesel livery. DAVID P. OROSZI

MIDDLE INSET No pot of gold; Amtrak's SDP40Fs fell short of expectations. JIM ASPLUND COLLECTION

BOTTOM INSET By decade's end, Amtrak's diesel paint scheme had entered "Phase II." ROGER PUTA

FACING PAGE TOP Amfleet and a P30CH make up the *Blue Ridge* at Cumberland, Md., in 1976. DAVID P. OROSZI

FACING PAGE BOTTOM Following withdrawal of the SDP40F fleet, the F40PH became the workhorse of Amtrak's long-distance fleet. In September 1979, F40PH 264 leads Train 31, the westbound *National Limited*, at Indianapolis Union Station. Along with several others, this train was discontinued the following month due to federal budget cuts. DAVID P. OROSZI

1981-1991

ABOVE **Amtrak's southbound** *Auto Train* **pauses for a crew change at Jacksonville, Fla., on January 25, 1984. The original, privately operated Auto-Train service ceased in April 1981, and Amtrak revived the Virginia-to-Florida overnight operation on October 30, 1983.** JIM BOYD; KEVIN EuDALY COLLECTION

LEFT **Train 19, the New Orleans-bound** *Crescent*, **departs Birmingham, Ala., on May 10, 1984. The former Southern Railway holdout had been an Amtrak operation since February 1, 1979.** DAVID P. OROSZI

BOTTOM LEFT **Built by a Canadian consortium, the LRC re-equipped VIA Rail Canada's corridor operation in the early 1980s but failed to make inroads in the U.S. after a two-year evaluation by Amtrak in New England.** JIM BOYD; KEVIN EuDALY COLLECTION

FACING PAGE TOP **The first Superliners — bilevel cars built by Pullman-Standard and inspired by Santa Fe's Budd-built Hi-Level fleet of the mid-1950s — entered revenue service in 1979. As deliveries continued into the early 1980s, they re-equipped all of Amtrak's western long-distance trains.** MIKE SCHAFER

FACING PAGE BOTTOM **Another Amtrak holdout, Denver & Rio Grande Western ended its** *Rio Grande Zephyr* **service in April 1983. In this April 1985 view its Amtrak successor, the** *California Zephyr*, **curves westbound through Byers Canyon in the Colorado Rockies.** W. SUNKEL; KEVIN EuDALY COLLECTION

passenger train annual 2021 67

1991-2001

FACING PAGE TOP **General Electric's Genesis-series diesels debuted in 1992 and quickly became Amtrak's new motive-power standard outside the Northeast Corridor. This pair of P42DC units leads Train 441, the** *Capitol Limited***, on CSX at Fairhope, Pa., on May 21, 1997.**
JOHN BARTLEY; KEVIN EuDALY COLLECTION

LEFT **Turboliner-equipped Train 248 at Oscawanna, N.Y., on May 14, 1991.** BRUCE C. NELSON

ABOVE **Amtrak acquired 20 GE P32-8BWH road switchers in 1991. Number 513 leads the** *Southwest Chief* **at Camden, Mo., on February 1, 1992.** DAN MUNSON

BELOW **Amtrak retired its original logo and branding in 2000, and introduced a new corporate identity built around the new "Travelmark" logo, described by Amtrak's brand management office as symbolizing "two rails that curve toward the horizon." Wearing the new livery, P42DC 46 and a mate lead the westbound** *Sunset Limited* **at Marana, Ariz., in 2003.**
S. MILSTEIN; KEVIN EuDALY COLLECTION

2001-2011

FACING PAGE TOP Amtrak introduced low-slung Talgo equipment on its Pacific Northwest *Cascades* service in 1994. In July 2005, F59PHI 450 powers Train 509 at Solo Point, Wash. SCOTT O'DELL

LEFT On the Northeast Corridor, Amtrak launched Acela Express service between Washington, D.C., New York City, and Boston on December 11, 2000. In August 2010, an Acela Express train led by power car 2004 cruises near Guilford, Conn. ROBERT A. LaMAY

ABOVE Headed to St. Louis from Chicago, P42DC 164 leads the Horizon Fleet cars of a state-supported Lincoln Service train across the Kankakee River at Wilmington, Ill., in June 2007. KEVIN J. HOLLAND

BELOW Shown here at New Haven, Conn., Amtrak's 40th anniversary exhibit train toured the system in 2011. GEORGE FLETCHER

passenger train annual 2021   71

2011-2021

LEFT A *Pacific Surfliner* skirts the beach at San Clemente, Calif., en route to San Diego on April 18, 2018. These trains operate on a 351-mile route serving communities on the coast of Southern California between San Luis Obispo and San Diego. ALEX MAYES

FACING PAGE BOTTOM Amtrak Train 5, the westbound *California Zephyr*, passes through picturesque desert scenery on Union Pacific's ex-Rio Grande main line at Thompson Springs, Utah, on September 28, 2019. ALEX MAYES

ABOVE Old and new in Baltimore: On June 18, 2021, a Siemens ACS64 electric locomotive leads the *Silver Meteor* (Train 98) out of the historic tunnels on the approach to Baltimore Penn Station. MARK GLUCKSMAN

BELOW Amtrak's new Alstom Avelia Liberty (Acela 21) crosses Pelham Draw in the Bronx, N.Y., on September 28, 2020, on its way to Boston. This was the first time the train had gone this far north on the line, as it was still in its testing stage. MARK GLUCKSMAN

Twilight for

Time is running out fo

In the eastern and northern suburbs of New York City, two regional commuter lines — Metro-North and Long Island Rail Road, both part of the Metropolitan Transportation Authority (MTA) — operated Budd Company electric-multiple-unit (EMU) cars known as M3s over their third-rail territories. LIRR removed its last M3s from revenue service in 2020, but M-N's cars will remain in service until sufficient M9 replacements are on the property.

A design that evolved from the M1 "Metropolitan" cars introduced by Budd in the late 1960s, the M3s are M-N's oldest operating multiple-unit cars.

Metro-North started using M3s in 1985. Operating from Grand Central

LEFT A westbound Long Island Rail Road M3 train slows for the station stop at Great Neck, N.Y., on its way to New York's Penn Station on May 7, 2019. LIRR's M3s carried their last passengers in 2020. JOHN LEVAI

ABOVE A northbound Metro-North M3 set arrives at Harlem-125th Street station in Manhattan's northern reaches on July 19, 2019. M-N's M3s will remain in service until sufficient M9 replacements arrive. JOHN LEVAI

the M3s

BY JOHN LEVAI

hese veteran Budd MU cars serving New York City

Terminal to serve the northern suburbs of Westchester and Putnam counties, M-N's M3s use the Hudson Line as far north as Croton-Harmon. On the Harlem Line, they operate as far north as the town of Southeast.

Of the two MTA operators, Long Island Rail Road used M3 cars the longest, beginning in the late 1970s. They could be seen on the Port Jefferson Line operating as far east as Huntington. On the Ronkonkoma Line, also known as the Main Line, M3s operated as far as Ronkonkoma. They covered trains heading to the Hempstead and West Hempstead lines as well, and put in plenty of miles on the Babylon, Long Beach, and Far Rockaway lines.

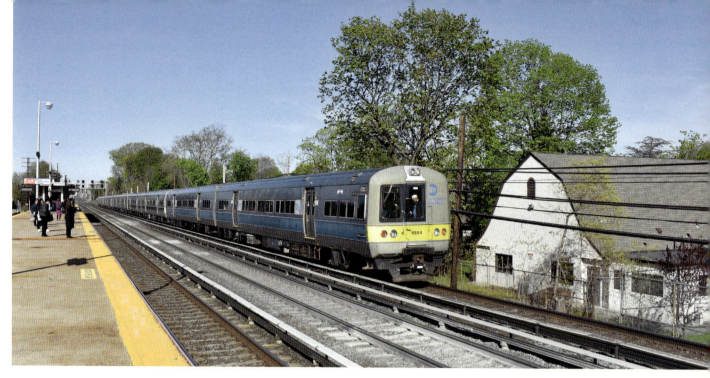

In recent years Metro-North and LIRR ran their M3s on weekdays, but newer M7 trains dominated the electric service of both railroads, especially on the weekends. It's not unusual to find M3s operating off-peak trips. Even though they can only be assigned to trains that operate in third-rail territory, that does not mean that there are assignments for any particular train to see M3s.

Metro-North M3s will continue to stick around for the short term. The M9 replacement order has been subject to repeated delays, resulting in M3s'

ABOVE A westbound LIRR M3 set heads away from the Bellerose, N.Y., station toward Jamaica and Manhattan's Penn Station on April 29, 2019.

BELOW Eastbound LIRR Train 410, employing an M3 set, slows for Flushing Main Street station in Queens on May 7, 2019.

FACING PAGE TOP An LIRR M3 set sits at the Port Washington, N.Y., terminus between runs on May 7, 2019. Note the end of both tracks' third-rail installation.

RIGHT Surrounded by massive commercial development as well as the endangered Nassau Tower and soon-to-be-replaced grade crossing at Main Street, an eastbound LIRR M3 train departs Mineola bound for Huntington on April 29, 2019. ALL, JOHN LEVAI

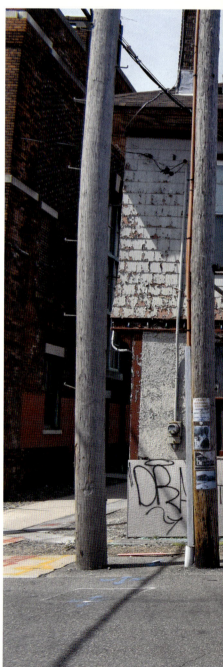

FACING PAGE TOP On May 7, 2019, an eastbound M3 set operating as LIRR Train 414 slows for the stop at Douglaston, N.Y.

FACING PAGE BOTTOM An eastbound LIRR M3 set heading to Port Washington bypasses the station at Bayside, Queens, on May 7, 2019.

ABOVE Heading for Port Washington on the same day, eastbound LIRR Train 418 crosses the Manhasset Viaduct between Great Neck and Manhasset.

LEFT Just as the sun is about to set, an eastbound LIRR M3 train running to Babylon from Manhattan races past the Valley Stream, N.Y., station on May 31, 2019. ALL, JOHN LEVAI

continued operation to the suburbs north of New York City.

During the last several years of operation, the LIRR M3s were showing their age, especially on the inside. There were worn-out seats, the walls and aisles were grimy, and ride quality was poor. Metro-North's M3s, on the other hand, are in better shape. Interiors are clean, the seats aren't ripped, and they provide decent ride quality. Despite the exterior look of what is essentially a subway car, the M3s can operate at speeds up to 80 mph. —continued on page 82

passenger train annual 2021 79

LEFT With the Hudson River visible at right, a northbound Metro-North M3 set on its way to Croton-Harmon slows for its stop at the beautiful and tranquil Scarborough, N.Y., station on May 24, 2019.

LOWER LEFT Taken from the south end of the Broadway Bridge over the Harlem River in Manhattan, a northbound Croton-Harmon-bound Metro-North M3 set runs alongside the Harlem River. The train is about to make its station stop at Marble Hill, Manhattan, on June 8, 2019.

ABOVE On May 24, 2019, a southbound Metro-North M3 set heading from Croton-Harmon to Grand Central Terminal is about to stop at Ossining, N.Y., with the former New York Central station building in the background.

BELOW Viewed from the Broadway Bridge, a southbound Metro-North semi-express train operating from Croton-Harmon to Grand Central Terminal departs Marble Hill station on June 7, 2019. ALL, *JOHN LEVAI*

An attraction of the M3s is being able to look out of the "railfan window" at the front and back of each train. Very few commuter railroads enable passengers to observe the tracks ahead and behind them while riding a regularly scheduled passenger train, but, for a while at least, it's still possible on M-N.

ABOVE **A southbound Metro-North Harlem Line M3 arrives at Harlem-125th Street on July 19, 2019. Next stop: Grand Central Terminal.**

BELOW **A northbound Metro-North M3 set at Harlem-125th Street on July 19, 2019.**

FACING PAGE TOP **Crossing the Lakeview grade grossing in Valhalla, N.Y., on June 14, 2019.**

RIGHT **In the late afternoon on June 14, 2019, a northbound M-N M3 set heads away from the old Kensico station in Valhalla, on its way to Southeast, N.Y.** ALL, JOHN LEVAI

time passages

New

Super Chief
Retaining its all-Pullman pedigree on a day when it was not combined with the *El Capitan's* coaches (in a 1958 cost-cutting move), Santa Fe's *Super Chief*, Train 17, winds through New Mexico in this early 1960s view. Highlight of the train's 1951 re-equipping was the Pleasure Dome, offering swivel chairs under glass and, on the car's main level, the celebrated Turquoise Room, which could be reserved for private dining. *JIM ASPLUND; KEVIN EuDALY COLLECTION*

Trains of 1951
Big Names and Lesser Lights

By 1951, the flood of all-new or substantially re-equipped postwar passenger trains in North America had slowed to a relative trickle. Indeed, the two trains that grabbed the most headlines that year were re-equipped versions of flagships that had already been given one postwar makeover: Santa Fe's *Super Chief* and Great Northern's *Empire Builder*. Elsewhere in the West, the SP/UP/C&NW *San Francisco Overland* also benefited from new streamlined cars, while in other parts of the U.S. the traveling public was being enticed by decidedly less-glamorous offerings, including no-frills Budd coaches on the Susquehanna.

Super Chief Six months after it was re-equipped on January 29, 1951, Santa Fe's premier train speeds through Illinois behind an A-B-B-A set of "Warbonnet" F-units. R.D. ACTON, SR.

BELOW Santa Fe's first dome cars (and the first of any railroad to operate between Chicago and Los Angeles) were built for the 1951 *Super Chief*. Unnamed but known as Pleasure Domes, the six Pullman-Standard cars were numbered 500-505. ROGER PUTA

TOP RIGHT The Turquoise Room, on the Pleasure Dome's main level, was a private 10-seat dining area that could be reserved en route and was a favorite of the *Super Chief's* regular clientele of Hollywood celebrities. ROBERT J. WAYNER COLLECTION

MIDDLE RIGHT The Turquoise Room in 1971, after a 1960s refurbishing. Tables have been partially set with Santa Fe's famed Mimbreño china. PHIL GOSNEY

BOTTOM RIGHT Pleasure Dome 504. The two low-level windows mark the location of the under-dome cocktail lounge. The Turquoise Room's two large windows are at right on the car's main level. In service, this end of the car was coupled to the train's dining car to facilitate Turquoise Room food service. ROGER PUTA

passenger train annual 2021 87

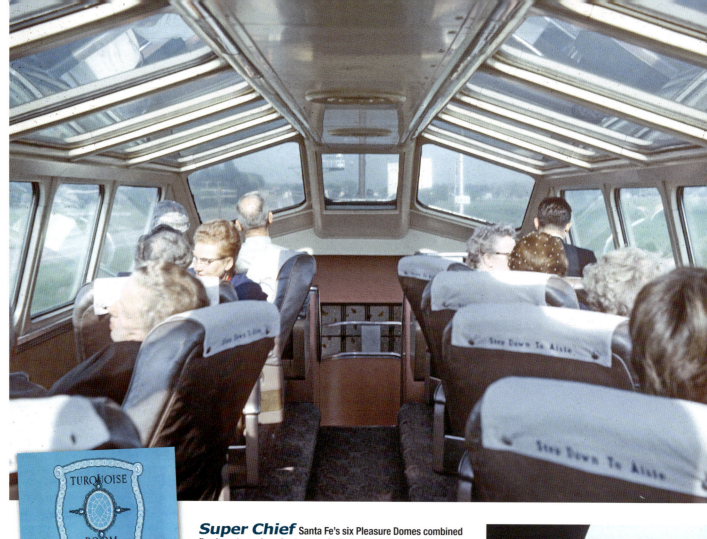

Super Chief Santa Fe's six Pleasure Domes combined fixed seats and parlor-type swivel chairs upstairs with lounge seating and the celebrated Turquoise Room downstairs.
KEVIN EuDALY COLLECTION; AD, KEVIN J. HOLLAND COLLECTION

BELOW On the main level of the *Super Chief's* Pleasure Dome cars, travelers could take advantage of the Main Lounge, shown here on the eve of Amtrak in 1971, as well as the Turquoise Room when it was not reserved for private use. A small cocktail bar — the Lower Lounge — beckoned under the dome. PHIL GOSNEY

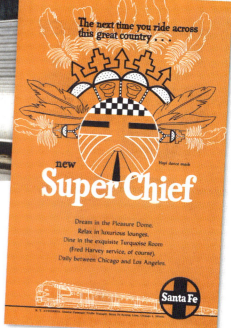

ABOVE Specialized cars require specialized maintenance, with Santa Fe employing this mobile washer at Albuquerque, N.M., in April 1958. Despite the modified fork-lift truck's extended reach, manual labor was still needed to clean the dome's uppermost glazing. JIM NEUBAUER; KEVIN EuDALY COLLECTION

BELOW In this 1957 view of the *Super Chief* at Los Angeles, sleeper-lounge-observation car *Vista Canyon* carries the train's drumhead sign. Built by Pullman-Standard in 1947 as one of four identical round-ended cars for that year's first postwar re-equipping of the *Super Chief*, all were retained after the train's 1951 upgrading. Five years later, the four *Canyon*-series observation cars were rebuilt with this square-ended configuration. Although an esthetic compromise, the change (with a standard diaphragm fixture to permit safe passage between cars) made it possible to run the cars, when necessary, in positions other than at the end of the train. Use of these rebuilt observation cars on the *Super Chief* was brief, ending in early 1958. KEVIN EuDALY COLLECTION; AD, KEVIN J. HOLLAND COLLECTION

Empire Builder/Western Star
Four years after it unveiled the first streamlined *Empire Builder* in 1947, Great Northern launched an updated "Mid-Century" edition of its flagship train on June 3, 1951. Debuting on the same day, GN's *Western Star* replaced the *Oriental Limited* as the railroad's secondary schedule between Chicago and Portland, Ore., with most of its equipment reassigned from the newly upgraded *Empire Builder's* 1947 castoffs. In this August 1956 view, *Tremperleau Mountain* (one of six observation cars built for the 1951 *Empire Builder* and reassigned to the *Western Star* in 1955) carries the latter train's neon tail sign. DON SWANSON; KEVIN EuDALY COLLECTION

BELOW **A 1951 publicity view of the new *Western Star*.** GREAT NORTHERN

FACING PAGE TOP **The Ranch was a heavily themed feature of the 1951 *Empire Builder*. The lunch-counter cars combined enough barnboard paneling, cowhide upholstery, and cattle-brand imagery to satisfy the most ardent dude rancher.** ROBERT J. WAYNER COLLECTION

FACING PAGE BOTTOM **Images of cowhide and cattle brands, including GN's own custom insignia, were featured on menus and decor for The Ranch.** MENU, KEVIN J. HOLLAND COLLECTION; ACF

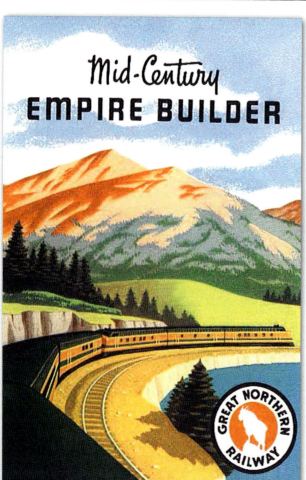

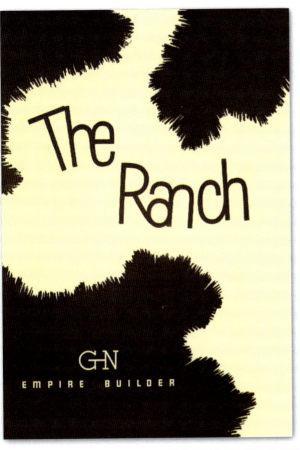

Empire Builder Bringing up the rear of the Mid-Century *Empire Builder* were distinctive tall-windowed *Mountain*-series sleeper-lounge-observation cars, from a group of six built by American Car & Foundry. Punctuating the *Empire Builder* until another re-equipping in 1955, they featured the train's name on their letterboards. After reassignment to the *Western Star* in 1955 (see page 90), they wore generic Great Northern lettering. Most of these cars' interiors were given over to lounge space, with a small bar, two roomettes, and an attendant's room in the forward end. Introduction of full-length Budd "Great Domes" in 1955 meant that the *Mountain*-series cars' lounge space was redundant, and the cars were replaced by *Coulee*-series observation-sleepers that had been rebuilt from the 1947 *Empire Builder's River*-series observation cars.

FACING PAGE The rear end of GN *Appekunny Mountain* at American Car & Foundry's plant in April 1951.

ABOVE Right-side builder's view of GN *Appekunny Mountain* prior to delivery.

LEFT AND BELOW Interior views of the forward and rear ends of *Appekunny Mountain's* observation lounge. Pier panels featured outline maps and official seals of the U.S. states and Canadian provinces served by GN.
ALL, AC&F PHOTOS. BARRIGER NATIONAL RAILROAD LIBRARY, ST. LOUIS MERCANTILE LIBRARY AT UMSL

Susquehanna After taking delivery of four RDC-1s from the Budd Company in 1950, New York, Susquehanna & Western re-equipped its locomotive-hauled New Jersey suburban services in 1951 with 16 stainless-steel Budd coaches. On June 12, 1956, steam-generator-equipped Alco RS-1 231 leads the four Budd coaches of Train 927 at Hackensack, N.J. WALTER ZULLIG

BELOW AND RIGHT Numbered 50-65, these spartan cars lacked air conditioning, but as some compensation for humid New Jersey summers had openable sash-type windows, 12 rooftop vents, and prominent interior fans. Each car had walkover seats for 133 passengers in a 3+2 configuration. After a decade in New Jersey, they were sold in 1961 for a second career in Saudi Arabia. In the view below, NYS&W coach 56 is at Butler, N.J., on January 29, 1961. At right, coach 54 was between trips at Jersey City in December 1956. BELOW, BOB GOIN; RIGHT, WALTER ZULLIG

Lehigh Valley RDCs The "Route of the Black Diamond" modernized its small-but-eclectic passenger fleet in mid-1951 with this RDC-1 and RDC-2 pairing, shown at Hazelton, Pa., on July 5, 1952. Replacing a steam-powered feeder service, the RDCs operated over the 26 miles from Hazelton to the LV main line connection at Lehighton. LV 40 became Reading Company 9163 in January 1962, and today this RDC-1 is preserved at the Railroad Museum of Pennsylvania. LV 41 had a long second career in Canada. The RDC-2 was sold to Canadian Pacific in 1958, becoming CP 9116. Rebuilt and renumbered CP 9306 in the mid-1970s, it went on to serve VIA Rail Canada as "RDC-5" 6143. JIM BOYD COLLECTION

RDCs overseas Although domestic orders for RDCs were relatively few in 1951, with LV the only new North American customer, Budd tapped overseas markets and built 22 RDCs for export during the year. A three-car order for Australia's Commonwealth Railways was loaded aboard ship at Philadelphia on January 22, 1951. Other RDCs built for export during the year included 16 for Cuba (11 RDC-1s and five RDC-2s) and three RDC-2s for the Saudi Government Railway. BUDD

tail end

Former Burlington Route *Denver Zephyr* dome-parlor-buffet-observation car *Silver Chateau* brings up the rear of Amtrak's *Abraham Lincoln* at Bloomington, Ill., in December 1975.
ALAN MILLER; KEVIN EuDALY COLLECTION